Raw Umber

Raw Umber

A Memoir

SARA RAI

First published by Context, an imprint of Westland Books, a division of Nasadiya Technologies Private Limited, in 2023

No. 269/2B, First Floor, 'Irai Arul', Vimalraj Street, Nethaji Nagar, Allappakkam Main Road, Maduravoyal, Chennai 600095

ISBN: 9789395767514

10 9 8 7 6 5 4 3 2 1

Typeset in Adobe Jenson Pro by Jojy Philip, New Delhi 110015

Printed at Parksons Graphics Pvt Ltd

For Lara, whose story this also is, and Vinoo,
who wanted me to tell it

Contents

Preface

This memoir has long been in the making. I feel as if I've always been writing it. It could be that once you are inside 'the thing', you can't keep track of time, which seems to stretch like elastic. Yet I have invariably found myself tied in knots. Setting down a sentence or even a word on the page immediately puts you in peril of losing your way. The word seems to demand after it another that you had not intended, and off you go, chasing after the rabbit as it disappears down the 'wrong' hole. It was the wrong rabbit anyway. The original thought with which you started out seems to have vanished.

Some of these pieces have existed in other versions for twenty years or more. They have remained, static and unbreathing, while the air around me changed. 'The Invented Father' and 'Lightfastness' formed a single essay, a little capaciously called 'About My Father', that I started writing while my father was still alive. But then my mother and her sister—my 'two mothers'—as well as my father died within the span of half a year. And the dead speak differently to you. 'The House of Fiction' seems to have lived, ever since I can remember, under my skin. It kept pushing up through the pores, reminding me of its presence, till I could finally turn to it. Then, once I had written about my maternal grandmother, my paternal granny Shivrani Devi, whom her husband Premchand referred to as the *yoddhastree* or 'warrior woman', began to insist that she be written about too. And there was my grandfather, Premchand. How could he be left out of the story? Since I had mentioned that my grandmother, my mother, my aunt, not to speak of my grandfather, all wrote stories, it felt necessary that I give my readers examples of their stories too. Some of these are included in the appendix to this book.

These essays that form a memoir about my family can also be read as stand-alone pieces though they are interconnected. It seemed worth doing to me, to take a look at the two places where my ancestors lived and where some lie buried. In a world of shifting certainties, this in itself seems a lot. The houses where I grew up reading and playing, the language in which I uttered my first words and which opened the world of the senses to me—such things have, to an extent, made me a stranger in the other places that I subsequently inhabited. They have felt like poor replacements.

The boundary between memory and fiction keeps getting blurred. There are things I remember, and others that I think I remember. In the quicksand of the past the ground moves constantly. I suspect that I have embellished a few facts, invented some details, and have paid the price of being a fiction writer. In the same way that while writing fiction I've paid the price of being a memoirist. All I can say is that I have been true to my own remembering of things. But then, remembering is also a way of imagining.

Since my fiction has primarily been in Hindi, while writing these essays I have dithered over which language to write them in. In fact, this 'language question' has always dogged me. In a recent podcast that I was invited to, my host was dismayed to find so little of my writing in English. I share his dismay. In some ways, these essays are also meant to correct the balance.

Sara Rai
July 2022

Palimpsest

There is something melancholy in the act of writing about one's past. This is especially the case if most of that past has taken place in the same house in which you still live. It is your family home—the house where you have always lived, and yet it is different. There were people who lived here, but many of them are no longer alive. Absent, they are still palpable. The air is saturated with their presence, their invisible script written into each corner of the house. You pull the door, and with a creaking of springs, it opens. The rooms are all there; you feel around you the weight of the air inside them, you know the pictures that were on the walls, the exact position of the furniture, the objects in the room; nothing has changed but everything feels changed. You remember the way light fell from the skylights, some of which are now blocked up or have disappeared in changes made to the house. There are cobwebs hanging from ceilings too high to be cleaned, not that you want to clean them. There are termites too, which swarm out of the ground and make mud tubes, reaching the most unlikely of places. You can, if you listen hard, hear the quiet clicking sounds they make as they move and munch away at the woodwork, hidden from sight. You want to disturb nothing. Each space in the house has a history, and it's as if everything in it casts a shadow, has a sort of ghost life. You try to catch the shadows, to pin them down. The harder you try, the more elusive becomes the business of shadows, and you come away with nothing.

You become obsessed with mirrors. Some mirrors are blind and reveal nothing. There are others in which you look and find in your face your mother or your grandmother. You see resemblances and patterns you had not noticed before. You hold up your hand to the mirror and look at the blue veins on it, that taper into the fingers with their neatly pared nails. The prominent, busy lines intersect and connect with the lesser ones, like so many rivers meeting with their tributaries on the triangular delta of your hand. With a start you realise that it is your mother's hand you are looking at. It is then that you know that you cannot ever be separated from your history. Your past is embedded in your body. But sometimes mirrors are false—distorted, damaged, or askew. These are the abstract mirrors, mirrors that you have imagined into being and that can play a trick on you.

There is a patch of black chillies in the garden—black leaves, deep mauve flowers, and the little chillies like black tongues. They look mysterious, with a hint of menace about them; watch out for those black tongues. They can put a hex on you. The black tongues curse and the curse comes true. You think of the chillies when you look at a photograph taken on Nauroz in the year 1971 in your mother's home at Nawab-ki-Deorhi in Banaras—you know that house well, for your history begins there. White was the colour for that year; it was the year of peace. Everyone in the photo is dressed in white, and all the food on the *dastarkhwan* is also white. You look at the faces in the photo and realise that all of those twelve people, except for you and your sister, are dead. There is nothing strange about that. Everyone dies. This is no narrative of loss. Dying is merely a function of living.

But then you see your mother. She is wearing a white sari printed with a paisley pattern in green. Short-sighted, she always wears glasses, and these particular ones have an onion pink frame. The family has gathered round the teapot in the front veranda of the house. Uncharacteristically, she does not participate at all in the conversation and a mysterious smile plays on her lips. Quite suddenly, with an absolutely impassive face, she winks. Only then do you see that the lens from that side of her spectacles is missing! It is a comic moment and everyone laughs, but it also brings home to you that there is much that you do not see.

Your father comes to you when you are not thinking about him. He is laughing. He does not speak. But he laughs. His laughter is loud and resonant, and the whole room rings with it. It flows down the stairs in a stream of gushing sound and it gathers in a pool at the bottom of the steps. It rests on the laburnum that is in full bloom, startling into flight a flock of roosting sparrows. His body shakes, his eyes fill with tears; it is not clear whether the laughter is happy or despairing. Then he stops all at once and is his solemn self once again. The laughter and then the stillness have the quality of something held in check just in time, arrested mid-air. It is like the angle of the sofa on which he sits; the precision seems to define his state of being. A knife-edge precision, almost.

One day you enter a room and find your brother sitting there. He leans back and closes his eyes as he does when he doesn't want to listen to what is being said. His wife is speaking. She is always speaking, a complicated web of lies floats just beneath her skin. For twenty-six years he has tried to get to the meaning of what she says, but the truth can just be glimpsed in flashes, for it can be found only in what she has not said.

None of this happens, of course. It cannot, because none of these people are here any longer. It's the mirror again, your personal mirror that keeps reflecting the past moments of which your life is composed. It invents some moments too, and you can never be sure if something really happened. The strange thing about living in the same house all your life is that you cannot go back to it, for you are still in it. And yet, you keep going back. It is not the house that you are returning to but a time; the house merely holds the accumulations of the years, evidence to the many layers of living in it that are transposed one upon another. You turn the things of the house over in your hands—threadbare fabric, rusty biscuit tins holding loose clattering buttons of all description, old watches that stopped long ago, opaque lamp chimneys, issues of *Lilliput* magazine yellowed with age—and you don't want to let go of anything, for those things, unbeknownst to you, have become part of who you are.

Sitting on the terrace you look about you. The *Argyreia nervosa* has spread its abundant foliage all over one side of the house. It's the elephant creeper. It grows rapidly, so quickly, in fact, that you feel it has grown another tendril or two in the moment that you looked away. You wonder if its roots go as deep into the earth as the plant does into the air. It has the house—and you—firmly in its grip. You shake yourself and try to leave. You've been trying to leave for years, fearing that in this stationary town with its two rivers and its narrow roads, you will become a pumpkin or a gourd. You look at other houses in other cities. Other lives flash across your mind. Hypothetical lives lived hypothetically. For you know that you will never go away. The house will never let you go.

Trombidium grandissimum

I cannot say that my relationship with Allahabad—the town where I live, and to which I have always returned as though my internal compass could point only in one direction—has been other than a tenuous one. For the town of Allahabad was merely the outer shell if our house on Drummond Road could be called the kernel. It seemed to exist simply as an extension of the space in which we spent our unhurried, unchanging days. Each day felt like the same day, so that our house wore the air of being located on a plateau of time where the past and the present had coalesced into a single block, and the future promised the same stasis. Yet the idea of stasis or of movement is only a way of looking, and places are often different from what they seem to be. In the slow days of my childhood, had I the ears to listen, perhaps I would have heard time rushing by with a sound like roaring water, flinging our house and its inhabitants headlong into the future.

Ours was not the only house where time seemed to stand still. This side of town had quiet tree-lined roads with large bungalows that had been built by the British when Allahabad was still the capital of the United Provinces. They gave the place a colonial look. Long shadows lay over the bungalows, and they were cast not only by the numerous tall trees. It was all nazul land where we lived, the site of eight villages that were razed by the British after the events of 1857. All those who had participated in the 1857 War of Independence, many of them Muslim landlords, had been hanged from the trees that grew on their properties and all along the roads. The Civil Lines and the Cantonment had been carved out of this land.

My father Sripat Rai had bought one of the bungalows in Civil Lines from Kathleen Emily Mills in 1948, not long after Independence. The Mills were a set of three siblings who had owned these bungalows, ours and the ones adjacent to it on both sides. Our bungalow was leasehold, as were the other two, with the lease starting in 1912 and valid for ninety-nine years. 6 Drummond Road, when my father bought it, was a row of high-ceilinged but rather dark rooms, the central one set up as a drawing room with a fire place and a mantelpiece of pale pink terrazzo. There was a veranda running the length of the house. The bungalow was set in a large parcel of land, with the servants' quarters at the back. In front of the house, when they bought it, there'd been a banyan which had aerial roots that reached the ground and colonised the space there, creating several rooms leading out from each other. It was a house in front of a house. The banyan was cut down, presumably to allow sunlight to enter our living room and the rooms that led off from it on either side. One of these that looked out onto the winding semi-circular drive had the best light and was used as a studio by my father who was a publisher and a painter, in the years when he was doing oils. He added a gallery behind the front rooms that was long as well as high, lined with a row of skylights near the roof that could only be opened and closed with the aid of long ropes. A mellow light entered the gallery, refracted as through a prism from the skylights, especially in the afternoon, when it made patterns on the walls. The gallery was an extraordinary feature of the house, rather grand in its absence of purpose, with bathrooms at its two ends. Then there were the rooms, added later, at the back of the house with their smaller appendages.

The first of the three rooms at the back was used as a dining room with a solid teak table in the centre and the reproductions of Picasso, Matisse and Bonnard that my father had brought back from his two visits to Europe, hanging high up on the walls, at the level of the skylights. A glass-fronted display case stood against the left wall, and among other knickknacks held the 'special' cups and saucers, decorative bowls and tureens, two glass decanters that my mother used for keeping sugar syrup, a round jar meant for fruit compote that had a pattern of apples, oranges and strawberries on its raised lid, and a twenty-four piece bone china dining set that was never used because of the anxiety that one of the pieces might break and spoil the set. A pair of salt and pepper cellars in the shape of small mynahs—black with yellow beaks—sat on the top shelf trapped behind the glass, forever denied the chance to fly. There was an old white Mena-Lux oven to one side in which my mother baked hot cross buns and gingerbread biscuits. The oven had two large drawers that opened forward on hinges, and it was in one of these that my mother would keep caramel pudding or kheer in five separate bowls, for us to eat when we came back from school. After one of my brothers died when he was thirteen, she'd forget and still set out five bowls. It was this Mena-Lux that would appear out of nowhere in my childhood nightmares in which I was being chased by someone. In the dream I would scramble to safety inside one of the drawers of the Mena-Lux, hiding in there till my pursuer had gone past. The Mena-Lux now sits in my kitchen. The knobs that turned the heat on and switched it off are stuck, and the wires at the back of the body are a tangled mess, yet I am reluctant to part with the oven that seems like a childhood friend. The drawers can still be opened, creaking on rusty hinges, and I look inside to find colonies of spiders.

Next to the dining room was my mother's room in which, as young children, my sister and I slept on a large takht drawn up close to her bed. There was a wooden chair fitted with a toilet pot that served as a thunder-box, which was conveniently placed in the gallery right in front of the room so that we may use it at night if we needed to, without having to wake up our mother. The third room in this row was another bedroom with a dressing room and a large toilet attached to it. The toilet was the best room with a view into the garden and a door opening outside through which the sweeper entered to clean the bathroom. A tender, somewhat discreet smell of shit hung about the small space partitioned off by a wall that did not go all the way up to the roof, and that held the two commodes, one Western style and the other Indian. In colonial times and for a few years after Independence there had been two dirt lanes on either side of the house. They were used by the municipal truck that came round to carry away the night soil from the bathrooms. This practice had stopped in my childhood and the two dirt lanes were soon incorporated into the land adjacent to the house. The commodes in the bathroom were connected by long pipes to cisterns made of cast iron set high in the wall. When you pulled the chain, a torrent of water gushed out into the toilet bowl making a terrific racket.

With five children to look after, the more or less permanent state of anxiety that my mother lived in was manifest in the medicines and unguents that she kept in the cupboard built into the bathroom wall. There was gentian violet and mercurochrome for the cuts and scratches we were prone to; one dyed the skin an exciting purple and the other bright red. There was iodine tincture and hydrogen peroxide, Nixoderm and Ascabiol lotion, Hakim Lookman's Lookman-e-Hayat oil, gaultheria oil, castor oil and eucalyptus oil, Joshina cough syrup and Vicks ointment, Iodex rub and Cibazol powder, Jawarish-e- Jalinoos, Amritdhara, Aqua Ptychotis, Agarol, and Isabgol for stomach indispositions, and Mandl's Throat Paint, most frequently in use because of our perennially recurring sore throats. My mother would snap a twig off the bougainvillea that grew right next to the veranda, fix on it a swab of cotton wool, dip it in the Mandl's and peer short-sightedly into the dark cavity of our mouth that she asked us to open wide and wider, till finally she was able to apply the paint to the painful throat. It was sweet and left an acrid aftertaste. And there was the marvellous cure-all apple cider vinegar that was sure to work when nothing else did. The cupboard bristling with medicines was her armoury against a malign fate that might, any minute, strike one of us down. But fate caught up with her anyway, her worst fear coming true when one of her sons, the twin older than his brother by six minutes, died at thirteen.

At a short distance from the bungalow was an outhouse that may once have been the kitchen but now consisted of a long room, a bathroom and a veranda. This unit was called the 'guest room', though no guests ever stayed there. Later it began to be called the music room when my mother used the place for her daily riyaz of Hindustani classical music. My sister and I also took our music and dance lessons there. Much later it became the office of the primary school that my mother set up in the premises of the house. By the end of its life, the 'guest room' had become Class IV. Like a soldier embroiled in a war against time, the room kept changing its battle fatigues, but destiny in the shape of monetisation eventually caught up with it when the land on which it stood was sold and the building demolished. The rubble lay there, getting bleached in the intense sun of several summers.

The past has been called another country, and perhaps it is, for the physical features of the town of my childhood have changed beyond recognition. Yet a similitude persists. The colonial names of the roads—Drummond, Hastings, Albert, Muir, Edmonstone, Elgin—have stuck, and despite the rapidly changing urban geography, they resist renaming. It is as if the names, belying the signposts, were written on the air itself. Although they branch out in different directions, all of them lead to the same place, which is the past. Unchanged are the relentless and dry summer months that give way to steamy monsoons, moistening my skin as with warm breath. The short winter months with their rapid elision into the melancholy I always associate with basant or spring in Allahabad. The grainy sound of the azan from a neighbouring mosque, seeming now near, now far, still hangs upon the dawn sky. And lapwings rise from stony outcrops calling out *Did-he-do-it? Did-he-do-it? Did-did-he-do-it?* as they have always done.

Drummond Road continues to be one of the most neglected and badly lit roads in the town, even though it is adjacent to Hastings Road on which is situated the Circuit House, originally the site of Revenue Courts during 'circuit tours' of the Board of Revenue. The old town is caught in the maw of the one it is becoming, but even the coming up, on this narrow road, of two sets of apartment blocks seven storeys high has not made a difference. That a few thousand people now live where earlier there had been a few dozen has led to an increase in noise and traffic but not to better lighting. In the sixties, Drummond Road was little more than a dirt track aspiring to be a road. At night a single yellow bulb glimmered at one end of it, battling the darkness. This bulb was regularly broken by lovers who met under cover of darkness, and the road stayed dark till the municipal corporation replaced the bulb after several months had gone by. Tall grass sprang up on both sides of the desolate road in the rains and was host to all manner of creatures: red and black ants, centipedes, millipedes, grasshoppers and scorpions. Frogs were everywhere, filling the night air with the sound of their croaking, and one had to be careful not to step on the snakes that could occasionally be seen sliding out of the grass. Ours was the second last bungalow on the right side of the road, inexplicably numbered 6, after which came 8. But if you were to count, there were only five bungalows on Drummond Road.

Number 8, the house adjacent to us on the right was a high-ceilinged affair like ours with jutting skylights and a chimney sticking out of the roof like a square thumb. There was a long line of rooms, let to tenants, at the back of the house beside a row of drumstick trees. Most of my information about the Mills came from the family barber who came regularly to our house, for there was always someone who needed a haircut or could be persuaded to have one. He had been around for a long time, and there was nothing he liked more than a good chat. Predictably, we called him Talkie, and in all the years that he kept coming to our house, no one cared to find out what his name was. He'd cycle into the compound, and having identified his quarry, slowly take off the iron-grey shervani that he wore on top of a betel-stained white kurta and pyjama and hang it on the nearest bush. Then, rather in the manner of a boa constrictor, he'd wrap his victim in a dirty white sheet that smelt of shaving cream and chewing tobacco and taking out his hair-cutting scissors that looked like a forked tongue, he'd set to work, telling tales of the white sahibs till the job was finished.

On a normal day, which most days were, no questions were asked of us and no answers expected. My siblings and I had the run of the place, and it was a large place with dark shadows alternating with brilliant sunshine, with pigeons settling on the skylights, thieving tree-pies with their long tails—threading the air in search of a nest with eggs or fledglings—dusky ravens and koels calling from the dust-coloured mango trees. One could call back at the koels and have the confused birds return the call, their voices rising in crescendo till they became quite hoarse. Then there were the frequent nocturnal visitors, civet cats, fruit bats, jackals straying from the riverside and occasionally, a porcupine. I never saw the porcupines but collected the quills they shed in the garden hoping to convert them into pens, though I had no idea how pens were made. Once, a fox turned up. It had hurt its leg and could not escape the curious eyes of us humans of whom it was, with reason, suspicious. We believed that at night witches with long hair and saliva-dribbling mouths sat on the midnight-blue neem trees, their skinny legs reaching the ground.

It was a gentle, self-contained world, yet it was located in the schizophrenic sixties. Barely a couple of decades after Independence, the country was beginning to realise that the euphoria was not going to last. The Indian army marched into Portuguese-occupied Goa in 1961; some important films—*Mother India, Mughal-e-Azam, Ganga Jumna*—were released; in 1962 the war with China took place, shattering India's self-confidence; and two years later, Nehru died. But caught up in our immediate, particular lives, we noticed little. The news of major events floated in as a distant echo, intent as we were on listening out for the thud of mangoes falling from the tree on hot summer afternoons, or in spring for the dove-like cooing of the green pigeons that sat in little flocks on the eucalyptus shaking their tails, and I waited to see if the birds known for never flying down to the ground would do so just the one time.

Kumar Cyclist would come round now and then, talking of the towns he had cycled to, the dusty roads and the long distances. It was not the places he'd cycled to that were important but the cycling itself. At the end of his description, he'd bow courteously and say, 'I request you to give me fifty rupees.' It seemed quite legitimate that we should pay him for cycling to places we did not know, for an activity that had nothing to do with us. There were two worlds, one within the gates of 6 Drummond Road in which things hardly moved except perhaps the clouds in the sky, and another world outside the gates that was in perpetual motion. It was from this world outside that a long-haired fakir came up to the gate every other day, playing the harmonium slung round his neck and singing Khusro's 'Mast Qalandar', or other songs by Kabir and Bulle Shah. My sister and I listened again and again to Connie Francis singing 'In My Heart There's a Signpost', and followed with excitement each twist in the tale of Prokofiev's *Peter and the Wolf* on the HMV gramophone that had come, along with a case of old records, from my mother's home in Banaras and had been placed on the pink terrazzo mantelpiece in the drawing room.

To get to the shops in Civil Lines you had to go past the Old High Court, the Head Post Office and the Gothic-looking Anglican Church. The busier parts of town lay beyond Civil Lines. I'd been there a few times, to the Clock Tower and to Chowk on a rickshaw. This side of town was dense and suffocating. There was a constant honking, buzzing, trilling, shouting, hooting—a whole universe of sound that fell upon my unaccustomed senses like a threat, and it was with relief that I returned to the quiet of our house. If I get the sense today that life was happening elsewhere while my siblings and I played Seven

Stones or Hide and Seek, and, as though with a foreknowledge of future events, games in which we pretended to die and then come alive again—now floating like a corpse on the pond in the garden and now coming back to life, now falling straight to the ground like a dead tree and scrambling up again—it is because it was. And yet—and yet. Who could have thought that we did not lead full, busy lives?

Once in a while something happened that took hold of our minds, if only for a while. One such instance was the 'miracle chapati'. This was a chapati-shaped fungus that multiplied overnight when soaked in tea and was supposed to impart to the infusion miraculous healing properties. Nobody found out whose research led to this discovery, but suddenly the air was thick with stories of cancer and other terminal diseases having been cured by the chapati-soaked tea. Newspapers carried pictures of the thing on the front page, and soon the chapati had found its way into almost every house. Our chapati too, arrived from the neighbour's, and my mother who had diabetes began to dream of days free of insulin injections. I had nothing to cure but myopia. I just watched the hideous mushroom multiply with fascinated disgust. I would put my finger to it; it had a cold and flaccid feel. It worked no miracles, however, and the fungus disappeared with the same suddenness with which it had arrived.

We slept outdoors on summer nights. Our beds were laid out in a row under the mahua tree, complete with mosquito nets and looking like a fleet of odd square ships on the high seas. The sheets were white and moonlight cool. We sometimes found ourselves trapped with mosquitoes inside the mosquito nets that were meant to keep them out. In the morning, we'd find the light-winged creatures dull with a surfeit of blood on the sides of the net. But mosquitoes were not the only light-winged creatures around. I remember the iridescent, powdery residue left behind on my finger from the wings of the butterflies we caught and with casual cruelty pressed between the pages of the 'butterfly book' while they were still alive. The small yellow ones hovering over the duranta hedge were the hardest to catch. While flipping through the pages of a natural history book, I found out that they were called clouded yellow or *Colias croceus*. There were other kinds listed in the book too, and some of them could be seen at our place—swallowtails and tree nymphs, admirals, monarchs, striped tigers and plain tigers, and small moths with gossamer wings—especially during the rains, when the humid heat in the garden attracted hosts of them. An old lemon tree stood near the pond at the side of the house and I squeezed the lemon rind into the pond, watching the colours that came into luminous existence when the oil in it met the water. I realised only much later that the sensory impressions gathered in a childhood of slowness sink in deep—deeper than memory. Unspeaking, they live inside you; they become your gut and your liver and your kidney. Maybe you don't know it, but they mould the person that you are, and it is they that keep you alive.

The bungalow adjacent to ours on the left was 19 Muir Road. It lay at the intersection of Drummond Road and Muir, which it faced. It had belonged to the Mills but was subsequently bought by the Raja of Nepal to provide accommodation for his son when he came to study at the university. The prince left after completing his studies, leaving the house in the care of Mr Singhal who continued to live in it with his family. Once in a while, Mr Singhal would emerge from inside, a stocky man dressed in wide-bottomed pyjamas and a white singlet that revealed hairy shoulders and made a striking contrast to his dark skin. He never spoke to us beyond the initial greeting.

He was fond of vintage cars and there were several parked here and there in the compound, slowly sinking into the earth. The house had two gates, atop whose posts were stone eagles that looked poised for imminent flight. The extensive compound of the rundown bungalow with its tiled roof backed into the frontage of ours, the two compounds separated by a hedge of thorny karonda bushes.

My sister and I found a gap in the hedge and regularly crawled through it into the grounds, completely overtaken by lianas and wild creepers, of the crumbling yellow bungalow. Mr Singhal had a son called Sudhir, who was my brothers' friend and a daughter Sandhya, my sister's and mine. Her nickname was Munni. She went to the same school as us, so we saw her every day. Munni was snub-nosed and dark, with her wavy hair tied in thin plaits swinging on her shoulders. She had a habit of speaking very fast and breaking into frequent laughter. Her mother rubbed *malai* on her face every morning, believing that cream taken straight off boiled and cooled milk had skin-lightening properties. A pair of Alsatian dogs, Tiger and Lily, could be seen snoozing on the massive sofas with solid curving armrests, in the semi-darkness of the drawing room. I never saw anyone else sitting on the sofas. The adjoining living room had a pantheon of Hindu gods arrayed on a shelf, and the whole place smelt of religiosity and curdled milk.

I crawled through the karonda hedge once, to find Munni with a stricken look on her face. She looked as if she were dying. She was bleeding to death, she said. She lifted up her skirt and showed me her panties that had a pattern of flowers on them. The blood on them also looked like an exotic flower. She said she was forbidden to go into the kitchen or touch the idols of the gods on the shelf while she bled, for she was 'impure'. But she confessed that she had touched them anyway and wanted to keep this a secret from her mother. We took slow turns around her house on the unpaved drive, breathing in the rotting smell of overripe guavas that had fallen off the trees near the moss-covered boundary wall. We talked about the Bavarian nuns at the convent school all of us went to. We wondered whether they ever took off their habits, what kind of clothes they slept in, what their hair was like beneath the wimple. Munni said she had seen a pair of very large bloomers and a commodious brassiere hanging on the line in the inner veranda of the nuns' living quarters. The information seemed shockingly intimate. It brought to mind what the bloomers and brassiere must contain, and in a nun those body parts seemed somehow sinful. For the nuns—Reverend Mother Hermine, Sister Seraphica, Sister Pia, Sister Johanna and Sister Elizabeth—seemed to be a species apart, with a crucifix dangling on a silver chain where their heart must be and the faint clean smell about them that seemed to signify more than physical cleanliness.

Classes were a routine affair, with lots of written work in which commas and full stops were dictated to us by the zealous nuns. Poems had to be learnt by heart and recited in an appropriately sing-song voice. Sometimes we had to parse lines of poems or whole paragraphs during a grammar lesson. One of the lines that I remember parsing was: 'The way was long, the wind was cold/ the minstrel was infirm and old.'

It was summer, a hot wind was blowing outside the large windows of the classroom, and I did not know what a minstrel was. The Angelus bell would ring at noon, three strokes repeated three times from the cathedral of St Joseph's, which was our 'brother school', where generations of Allahabad boys had studied. The bell announced prayer time for the nuns and lunch break for us, and the girls would stream from the classroom, calling out in high excited voices '*Bellring baj gayi!*' 'The bell-ring has rung!'

The girls called the toilet 'fairyland'. This was a rank and seedy grey cement structure that stood apart from the main building of the school. It would be dark inside. While entering it, one had to guard against stepping on foul, wet, and squishy substances. In fact, one tried not to enter it at all. It was where you could expect to encounter grossness in unidentifiable forms—pushed up against the wall, I found a bloodied sanitary napkin that looked like the leg of a dead animal before I figured out what it was. Phyllis, an exchange student from East Lansing, Michigan, had an 'accident' in class simply because she was trying to stay away from this chamber of horrors. Another friend was expelled from school for creating 'dirty' graffiti on its walls. Why does this sad building that the students avoided going to push its way up in the storehouse of my memory? Perhaps it is because it formed the setting for a shared childhood experience of revulsion, and of the shameful realisation that the human body, stripped down to the fundamentals, amounted to shit and piss and blood, and that it was mortal.

There were books locked away in glass-fronted cupboards in the school classrooms, and when we ever got hold of them, one book every fortnight in the library period, we came away with *Little Women* by Louisa May Alcott, Susan Coolidge's *What Katy Did* and *What Katy Did Next*, or *Lorna Doone* by R.D. Blackmore. There were no books in Hindi in the classroom library, and we were discouraged from speaking in Hindi. Miss Williams was the needlework teacher. She was a crotchety Anglo Indian who wore her iron-grey hair in two thin plaits that were wound round the top of her head and the hair looked like it was made of wire. She dressed in long skirts that reached below her knees, to set an example to the girls whose tunics she thought were too short. All one could think of during her class were the various kinds of stitches that she had taught us to embroider—herringbone stitch, stem stitch, cross-stitch, lazy daisy or French knots. In the music period, Sister Elizabeth, a German from Bavaria with a beaming ageless face, played the piano and taught us to sing 'Stille Nacht, Heilige Nacht', 'Come All Ye Faithful' and 'Hark the Herald Angels Sing'. Many of the girls lip-synced with the others, and it was a terrifying moment when you were asked to sing on your own.

I hadn't realised that telling lies was a sin. It was just something you did, and I found nothing wrong with playing around a bit with the facts. But then the moral science period happened. I was suddenly aware of 'sin' and 'atonement', and I began to feel uneasy at the smallest acts of transgression I committed, and they began to impinge on my guilt-free life. We were warned against even briefly touching a boy's hand, let alone holding it, for the fall into depravity was sudden, swift and irremediable. Inside the gates of St Mary's Convent existed a different moral universe, and only faint echoes of the local immediate world of Allahabad filtered into the pindrop silence of its old stone corridors.

I shifted to Delhi to attend college a few years later and lost touch with Munni, who remained in Allahabad, teaching in the same school where we had studied, writing sporadically for the local newspaper, the *Northern Indian Patrika,* until she married and moved away. I ran into her many years after that, when she was getting off a rickshaw in front of her house. Except for her lips that had turned a light pink, she looked the same. She recognised me instantly. She had by then developed a form of dementia in which she had trouble remembering the people whom she'd met recently, though her memory for things that had happened long ago was intact. 'I know *you*!' she said when she saw me. Apart from that one meeting, it would be twenty years before I met her again. Her brother had died, as had mine. We had grown old, a whole lifetime had gone by, but her mother was still around. 'Don't tell Maiya!' she whispered to me. She remembered well the day on which she'd told me about her first period. The years had done nothing to cloud that memory, though she hadn't registered the fact that I still lived next door. Later, when I took her mother's bony hands in mine, I felt like I was holding a bunch of cold metal keys. I didn't tell her Munni's secret. When I heard the news of Munni's sudden death last year, as intriguing as her life had been, I thought of the secret that she had carried with her to the pyre.

Beyond our house, immediately to the right and in front of Number 8 was a deep nallah whose furrowed sides were composed entirely of the town's garbage transported there by the municipal corporation in enormous overloaded trucks. The smell of the decomposing garbage lingered in the air after the truck had gone, and sitting on the veranda, reading Enid Blyton or Agatha Christie, we'd hold our noses so as not to breathe in the foul air. In the sixties, a dry wilderness fanned out across the land beyond the nallah, tapering on to the kachhaar, the flood plain of the river Ganges. The village of Nivada lay just before the kachhaar began, with huts on a low escarpment made of garbage. Whole families of swine lived on this stretch. When dealers in pig products cut their bristles to make brushes, their screaming would be heard up to our house. The pigs, obese and black with the muck from the nallah they wallowed in, were butchered. Our cocktail sausages came from the Aligarh Central Dairy Farms outlet in Civil Lines. We imagined the pigs at those farms to be pink and squeaky clean.

In a good rainy season, the Ganges could look like an ocean. It could creep up into the nallah. There would be boats on the water, ferrying the people whose homes had been flooded, usually very poor people from Nivada. Even now the river occasionally swells its banks, and flood-affected people take shelter in schools and other public buildings. But for most of the year it recedes far back and morphs into a silver thread. In my childhood, we could see the river from the roof, a blue-grey line at the end of a vast tract of stubbly wasteland. Tall buildings have come up since then, blocking the view of the Ganges. Sometimes my sister and I would go up to the roof at night. There was nothing to see but darkness. It could have been the edge of the world. It could have been the sea, where eagles sat on pointed crags, and on which ships set sail for distant ports.

Kedarnath comes to teach us kathak. He wears a kurta-shirt and a stainless steel bangle on one wrist. He is a short man who chews paan continuously. He makes slapping sounds with his feet on the smooth cement floor of the music room as he shows us the steps, with a force and precision that is impossible to imitate. My sister dances and dances, her skirt whirls when she turns round and round in circles twelve times without stopping. Soon she can do sixteen circles, and her waist length plait too whirls with her. I sit down on the floor and refuse to dance. I tell my mother to get my name cut off the list of students, though there are only two students, my sister and myself. Kedarnath takes the silver wrapper from his packet of cigarettes, forms it into a cup and puts a dab of lime from his betel box on the base of the cup. He throws it up at the ceiling. Sometimes the cup sticks to the ceiling, sometimes it doesn't. It's a hit-or-miss operation. My sister and I clap when it sticks. Ustad Dilshad Hussain comes to give us lessons in Hindustani classical singing. He starts us off with Raga Yaman. He has henna-dyed hair and a thick bullish neck from which issues a thin rasping voice. I resist the singing too.

Maulvi Sahib has his quarters at the back of the house, which means that he can arrive for a lesson at any time, and it always seems to be time for a lesson. He is called Talib Jaipuri and he teaches us Urdu. He is a shrunken, slightly bent old man who always wears a shervani and is an innocuous sort of person, or so we think. But then he starts rapping us sharply on the knuckles with a pencil for work not done. We find out a few months later on our return from Ranikhet, where we'd gone for the summer, that he accidentally knocked over a kerosene lamp in his room and died in the fire that broke out. His shervani still hung on an iron hook in the charred room. It was all that had survived. The room is whitewashed and Abdul Mali moves in. He's our gardener. He is slightly deaf and wears a bidi that I have never seen him smoke, tucked behind his ear. There seems to be a mysterious connection between his deafness and the bidi behind his ear. They are linked in some way that I cannot fathom. He believes that there is a serpent flying in the sky. If it bites you get paralysis and then have to be taken to the red room, which is what he calls the ICU. One day he tells me that if you preserve a cat's placenta, dried and shrunk, in a box, misfortune won't come near you. The distinction, for me, between an imagined world and the real one gets blurry.

I start chewing leaves, different ones, to find out how they taste and also which ones can kill. I don't die. There is the fascination of making a spider crawl up your arm. Of trying to understand the language of garden chameleons as they bob their sinister crepuscular heads, and the evening sky turns from orange to pink and gold. The shallow water-race that runs round the house gets blocked with leaves when the trees shed them in March. From under the leaves appear striped skinks, dangerous exotic-looking centipedes and shiny green beetles, ancient and indestructible forms of life. Then there are the red velvet mites or rain bugs. They come out of the ground only after the rains. I make nests of leaves and grass and place the shy creatures in them, their red showing up starkly against the green. *Trombidium grandissimum*. The local name for them is birbahuti. The rain bugs have since disappeared—as have most of the bungalows in Allahabad.

The Ancestor in the Cupboard

He was the unbelievable figure in the family cupboard that no one had seen. No one except for my father who was twenty years old when Premchand died, my uncle who was then fifteen, and my grandmother who'd been married to him for thirty years and outlived him by forty. He'd already been dead twelve years when my parents got married, so there was no question of my meeting him. Yet I saw him everywhere. The air of our house was permeated with my grandfather's presence. His life of commitment to the underdog, his willingness for personal sacrifice for the larger good and his ideals all of these were woven into the texture of our lives even if no one talked about him. But we did talk about him. For instance, when my siblings and I complained about the power cuts that were frequent in my childhood, especially during exam time, we'd be told to think of him who read and even wrote by the light of a dhibri, a small oil lamp. Swotting over our textbooks, we'd think with envy of what we'd heard about his first school, a madrasa in Lalpur, half a kilometre away from Lamahi. The maulvi, with his passion for birds, had bulbuls, mynahs and munias in cages that hung everywhere in the school. The students would be sent out to gather worms for the birds, and these outings turned into nature walks. Walking in hushed silence down the stone corridors of the convent school in Allahabad where I studied, my mind would wander. My grandfather's school sounded much more fun than my own.

If one of us failed a maths test we'd be scolded at home, but we knew it was a mock scolding. For beneath it all there was an unstated pride, for 'his' maths had been weak too. In fact, he failed to clear a qualifying entrance exam for college because he was stumped by the maths test. Even in his shortcomings he was a role model that we proudly emulated. He'd be remembered when arvi or baigan was cooked, for these were some of the vegetables he'd been advised not to eat because of his poor digestion. We'd laugh at stories about his childhood pranks, for instance the time when he had nicked a friend's ear while giving him a haircut in a game in which they were pretend barbers. Or, there was the incident where he and his cousin had stolen a rupee. The money had come in from the sale of hemp, and had been kept in a niche high on the wall. They stole the money but didn't know how to spend it. Naturally they couldn't get away with it. He later wrote a story about the incident, called 'Chori'(The Theft).

My grandmother, Shivrani Devi, once in a while, narrated incidents from his life. One of them was about the harkara or mail-runner, Kazaki. Premchand's father worked in the postal service in Jamaniya. Kazaki would bring the child gifts of sugarcane, guavas and carrots, and give him a ride on his shoulders. It cost Kazaki his job when he was late coming in for work one day, because he'd gone looking for something he wanted to give the boy. The incident left a mark on Premchand and he would later write a story about him. How could a person run for miles over difficult terrain, all the while carrying letters and parcels and sometimes money? Leading a comfortable, mostly sedentary life, as I did, this sounded to me like too much exercise. But the image stayed with me—the harkara wearing his red turban and badges, armed with a spear for self-defence and bells to announce his arrival. It was rather dramatic.

Then, there was the incident about the five rupees worth of gur. He'd been sent to Banaras to study and his father had sent him five rupees to buy gur. The jaggery was supposed to keep up his strength for the approaching exams. He was also, at the age of fifteen, about to get married. His father, rather too optimistically perhaps, must have thought that the supply of gur would last him till the exams. There was little chance of that. Premchand, his cousin, and a few other friends now discovered in themselves a compulsive appetite for gur. The stocks started depleting. After several unsuccessful attempts at hiding the key to the sandook that held the gur, my grandfather finally threw the key into a well. My grandmother laughed when she told us these stories. This in itself was rather unusual, for she was not given to laughter.

Our father never bought us new shoes till the old ones were completely worn out. He always asked to see our battered shoes before we could make a trip to Civil Lines to buy new ones. My grandmother would say he'd taken after his grandfather. Premchand's father, when he had to buy shoes for his son, always bought the inexpensive chamraundhe joote, rough leather shoes made of cattle hide that had been cured and treated with salt. They were always bought from Andhrapul in Banaras and the price never exceeded twelve annas.

My grandmother would look disapprovingly at the tailor who'd set up his work station in our back veranda. He was there to stitch clothes for us that she regarded as extravagant, and commented that her husband never bought cloth that cost more than four annas per metre.

There he was, in a yellowing photo on a shelf in the living room, a small figure dressed in a white dhoti and kurta, a cap of rough cloth on his head and a hole in his left shoe that he appeared to be oblivious of. Perhaps these were the chamraundhe shoes that he continued to wear long after his father was gone. The photo of him wearing torn shoes had become well known because of the essay 'Premchand ke Phate Joote' (Premchand's Torn Shoes) that the satirist Harishankar Parsai had written. They were hard on the feet and pinched, but he was by now used to them. His wife, also small, wearing Gandhi spectacles and khadauns on her feet, sat beside him. A kindly, rather shy smile was starting up on his face, and it made you wonder about who he really was, behind the very public persona that he had acquired. He'd been fifty-six years old when he died. It felt odd now to be older than one's grandfather. In death he'd always remain young, younger than the rest of us. His absence from our house was an emptiness peopled by the idea of Premchand, for Premchand himself was missing. And the idea of him was ubiquitous, not confined to just our house.

He could appear from anywhere, and he was a shape-shifter. One day he'd be the ventriloquist-clerk at the bank you went to, from whose mouth issued Premchand's voice reciting lines from his stories. Or suddenly he would transmogrify into the man sitting across from you in the train—dirty white kurta, a gamchha wrapped round his head—who remembered entire paragraphs from my grandfather's work. Then there was the watchman who sat outside the gate of the school my mother ran for years. He would often be seen reading a grubby volume of Premchand's stories, and he sometimes spouted from it a line or two that had particularly impressed him. The man was difficult to get away from. We'd be invited to performances of plays based on his stories, most often 'Idgah' or 'Bade Bhai Sahab' (Elder Brother). The extreme reverence with which our family was met left in me a confused mix of pride, embarrassment and guilt. For what had we ourselves done to deserve this attention?

And what exactly was it that made him so popular? Perhaps it was his voice, compassionate, generous, and funny, that spoke to the particular reader and each reader was the particular reader. The fact of how loved he was, came home to me again when I travelled to his village, Lamahi, in 2005, to attend a function to celebrate his 125th birth anniversary. We followed the road that leads out of Banaras towards Azamgarh, and which goes past the tehseel of Pandeypur, itself now an extension of Banaras. Continuing straight on this road, you reached Sarnath. But before Sarnath, the road, now called Munshi Premchand Marg, bifurcated and narrowed as it wound to the village of Lamahi. Trees—mahua and mango—lined both sides of the road. Fields of sugarcane stretched away. There'd be mustard in winter. So soon after Banaras, suddenly it was as if you were deep in the countryside. The village itself had changed little but for a few more pukka houses and shops. It was now included in the municipality of Banaras. But it was still a village.

The house he'd built still stood there, but just about. The roof had caved in and the little room where he was born had been pulled down. The site of his birth was marked by a memorial bust that bore little resemblance to my image of him. The bamboo grove near the house was filled with the chirping of birds. There was a pond that had no water. The Ramlila ground was the same; it was the setting for at least one of his stories, and I was keenly aware of this as I walked around. I remembered from an earlier visit an ox-driven oil press, an ancient looking machine to which an ox was yoked. The ox walked heavily, round and round in circles, the movement working the machine to yield oil from the mustard crop that had come in. There was a well with decaying vegetation on the brick lined inner wall. A makeshift stage had been set up, and several very large canopies were in place over the whole area to provide shelter from the scorching July sun. A couple of ministers from the state and central governments were expected and their late arrival delayed the proceedings.

What I couldn't stop looking at was the crowd. Many people sat under the canopies, and some on the ground outside where there was no shade—people sitting huddled close together in the area that had been cordoned off. They seemed to have been waiting there patiently for hours. Who were these people? Why were they there? Were they all readers of Premchand? Some of them must have been. But many would have been illiterate and not known how to write even their own names. They could have been characters from a Premchand story themselves. Had they come just to view the spectacle, because something was happening in the small village where nothing happened? They rarely got to see such important people as were coming for the event. The reasons for the gathering could have been many, but over and above everything, it seemed to me that they were there simply to pay homage. To a writer who they perceived not as some distant intellectual, but as one of their own—who had found their stories, above all else, worthy of telling, who had put them on the literary map to make them count for something.

To get to the heart of Premchand's enduring appeal, it is important to see this shift in perspective that came with his writing, the redefining of the stage of fiction and the actors in the lead roles. His world is inhabited by common people. Men and women who live out their lives in poverty, in a system that spares no one. Women have a crucial role in his fiction; they are credible and strong characters, quite often decision makers who influence the resolution of the story. Dalit, tribal and upper caste, Muslim and Christian live and breathe as themselves, without coming across as mouthpieces of particular ideologies. Of course, he's had to face the music for this. The fact that he used caste names, simply occupational categories in his work, is now construed to be derogatory. His treatment of dalit characters is always sympathetic; one could even say that he swings to the other end of the pole, and with his bias in their favour, he portrays them as victims. This is what some dalit readers and intellectuals now strongly object to. His stories have a natural earthiness that was quite missing from literature at that time. Is this then—his moving fiction into the real world—where his greatness lies?

Premchand's own view on all of this was: 'What is there in my life that I can talk about? It is a featureless, plain sort of life, the kind that millions of people lead in this country. A common householder caught in the problems of domesticity, a poor school teacher who kept pushing the pen all his life in the hope of some gain which did not come. What is extraordinary about any of this? I am like a grass reed swaying by the river and the wind makes sounds within me. That's all there is to it. I have nothing of my own ... my story is the story of the winds that sang within me ....'

He caught the 'story of the winds'. Premchand himself was a voracious reader of the fantasies and romances current at the time. He talks about it in 'Meri Pahli Rachna' (My First Literary Work). Some of the much-read Urdu novelists of the time were Maulana Sharar, Pandit Ratan Nath Sarshar, Mirza Hadi Rusva and Maulvi Muhammad Ali of Hardoi. There was Maulana Faizi's encyclopedic *Tilism-e- Hoshruba* and also Urdu translations of works by popular Victorian writers like George W. Reynolds who wrote city mysteries or 'penny dreadfuls'. The most famous of these was a long narrative about the seedy underbelly of mid-nineteenth century London called

The Mysteries of London. At the time, his father was posted in Gorakhpur. He was thirteen years old, studying in Class 8, and he describes how he would read these books at Buddhilal, the bookseller's shop. Since he couldn't sit there all day reading books, he started selling guide books and notes from the shop to the children at the mission school where he studied, in return for which he could take some of the books home. He read hundreds of novels in this way, and one can see how a creative universe was beginning to gather shape within him, a forming of opinions on literature and its role in society.

He soon became interested in writing. 'I would write and tear it up, write and tear it up,' he says about that time. The first piece he wrote at the age of thirteen was a play, and it was lost soon after it was written. It was about an affair between a distant uncle of his and a lower caste woman—he was settling scores with the uncle who frowned upon him for reading novels. He read the piece out to his friends to much hilarity. This 'eye for an eye' sort of writing was something that he would never return to. Rather he became serious about the role of the writer. It was the writer's job to focus on the problems of society. But who would read such well intentioned, didactic writing? The work would first have to be entertaining in order to be read at all. How could it further any cause if it was dull and preachy? But at the same time, frivolity and sensationalism were to be avoided. In all his musings about literature with a purpose, what exactly was he fighting against? Corruption was rife then, as it is now, and there was a sharp caste and class divide with its consequent exploitation. There was no getting past indebtedness and money-lending. Then there was the malaise of untouchability, not to speak of the appalling condition of women, particularly widows—and all these problems were compounded by the presence of the British in the country.

So much to be written about—yet all that did get written were improbable tales of magic and romance. They went against the grain of his ideas about literature—in elaborating on these ideas, he does preach now and then. He had so much to say, and he was in a hurry to say it. All of his stories don't quite make the mark, and need to be looked at as part of a changing, seeking imagination. He took the *technique* of writing a gripping tale from the Urdu dastans that he so enjoyed reading, and turned it to his own ends. The stories swing wildly from the didactic to depictions of psychology, from farce and irony to tragedy. He is never lacking in empathy for his characters; he looks at them from the inside. Each character's point of view is presented so that even the darkest characters seem to be the way they are because they are driven by circumstance and not because they are intrinsically evil.

In the meantime, he got married. He'd been married once before; a marriage arranged by his step-mother's father when Premchand was fifteen years old. It was a disaster. In 1905–6, my grandfather married my grandmother who was a child widow. This was a time when widow remarriage was almost unheard of. My grandparents' marriage certainly endorsed his views on the subject and, it might be added, also hers. He'd been struggling a little just before. His father had died, leaving him to look after his step-mother and her two sons. They were desperately poor and he was the only one bringing in money. He found work as a private tutor to a lawyer's son on a salary of five rupees. He sent home three and lived off the other two. He had a lucky break when he got to teach at a small mission school at Chunar in 1899. The salary was eighteen rupees, a sum he would never have dreamt of. He kept changing jobs, but he was also writing. Premchand, during the years 1905–20, published a lot on political and social issues in the Urdu periodical *Zamana* brought out by Munshi Dayanarayan Nigam from Kanpur.

I grew up hearing about how, in 1920, in response to Gandhi's call for non-cooperation, my grandfather, forty-one years old and a father of two young children, resigned his job in the education department, with no idea how he was going to look after his family. He was in Gorakhpur at the time of Gandhi's visit to the city, and was much moved by what he heard him say. The result was that he and his friends started selling charkhas, to encourage the making of the home-spun cloth that Gandhi had been talking about. This was in keeping with Premchand's determination to live out in his own life the causes that he believed in. It cast him in a light that was rather saintly. He felt like a mythic figure. But then there was his laughter. Loud and infectious, his laughter was the one thing that had been inherited both by my father and my uncle, who were quite different from each other in most other things. When my uncle came to our house in Delhi, there'd be times when the brothers would laugh at the same time, and along with theirs, one heard the echo of a third laughter, their father's.

The memory of my early encounters with my grandfather's books is hazy. To start with, there was the feeling that I had somehow imbibed his writing through a sort of hereditary transfusion. The only stories I'd read were the ones prescribed in the Hindi syllabus at the Catholic convent school where I studied. Everything else was taught there in English by German nuns with a grim sense of purpose. There were the children's stories too—*Jangal ki Kahaniyaan* (Jungle Stories), or *Kutte ki Kahani* (A Dog's Tale), several copies of which lay around the house. Somehow for me they lacked the sparkle of 'Do Bailon ki Katha' (A Tale of Two Oxen) or 'Poos ki Raat' (A January Night), both of which also had animals as the key characters.

The novel I first noticed at the age of about eleven or twelve was *Godan*. It was a glossy, greenish volume that looked back at me in eye-level contact from one of my father's bookshelves. Oddly enough, it was not in Hindi or Urdu but in a strange language that I then thought was Norwegian; it turned out to be Danish. This was the complimentary copy sent by the publisher to my father. And now my memory plays a trick on me. I thought I remembered on the cover a picture of a farmer with his cow. But when I saw the book again recently, somehow the farmer and his cow had turned into a large-eyed woman standing against the backdrop of a village! I remembered leafing through the pages of this version in my childhood, adrift on a sea of incomprehension in which the one word 'Godan' written in Roman as well as in Nagari shone like a beacon. Some years later, I found, on a shelf in the books godown at our place, several copies of the original Hindi version, first published in 1936. There was also an Urdu version that appeared after his death, as well as a copy of Gordon Roadarmel's *The Gift of a Cow*, published by Allen and Unwin in 1968. So, I read the Hindi version of the book, generally considered his masterpiece, as an adult, and by then at a comfortable distance from the complicated feelings I was prey to in my childhood and teenage years.

Premchand wrote *Godan* intermittently over a period of about three years, a time when he had many things on his mind. There were niggling problems with Saraswati Press, which had run into financial difficulties; he'd also started the Hindi magazine *Hans* in 1930, and a journal on political affairs, *Jagran*, in 1932. In April 1934, he had been enthusiastically summoned to Bombay by Ajanta Cinetone. He signed a contract to write film scripts and even had a minor role in the first of his stories made into a film, *Mill Mazdoor*. The film was released in Lahore but was later banned as it had instigated factory workers to rebel against mill owners. In an ironic twist, the film inspired the workers in Premchand's penurious Saraswati Press to organise a protest too, when the bankrupt enterprise had been unable to pay out the wages. The move to Bombay didn't turn out to be such a good idea after all, and Premchand was back in Lamahi before the year was out.

He was working on *Godan,* though he wasn't in good health. It was not surprising, then, that *Godan* took so long to finish and was published only a few months before he died in October 1936. It might also explain, to an extent, the uneven quality of the narrative and the fragmented structure of the novel as a whole. *Godan* is a political novel written at a time when the freedom struggle was at its height, and Premchand's failure to mention the British presence is ironic, if a little mystifying. His fascination with the figure of Gandhi as a moral and political force, if not immediately obvious, certainly infuses the spirit of the novel. *Godan* was his last published work. He left behind an unfinished novel, *Mangalsutra,* which was his last book. But *Godan* was the first novel by Premchand that I read.

How was I to make sense of my grandfather's virasat, the inheritance that I had been born into? A couple of years ago, I was approached by someone who wanted to set up a Premchand museum. He asked if the family owned any objects that had belonged to my grandfather, which could be donated to the museum. There was nothing. Is it possible to represent, in material terms, a life so devoid of personal possessions? How was a museum to be planned around a life that was so indistinguishable from that of the common man? I could see him looking at me from his photograph that I keep as a lucky totem above my writing desk that had once been his—it's the one thing he owned that is now with me, something that I am unwilling to give away, even to a museum. And the photograph was the same one my siblings and I had argued over when we were children. Our pride in our ancestor reached absurd levels at times. We searched the face in the photo for family resemblances and came to the conclusion that my brother looked the most like him. But I too wanted to look like him! He had high cheekbones, slightly slanting eyes and rather prominent eyebrows. His left eyebrow, I decided, was definitely like my own.

I looked at him again. Had he just winked at me?

Warrior Woman

She seemed always to be walking.

Her wooden sandals would clatter through the large and empty house with thirty-six rooms in Godowlia. The khadauns were made of sheesham wood and had a single strap of coarse cotton across the top, in which her knobbly feet nested like two boats anchored in a harbour. The wood of the sandals was smooth, so that it must have been difficult for her feet to find purchase, but she was used to them and she walked all the time, easily and noisily. Whenever she visited us in Allahabad, she'd walk every day to my uncle, Amrit Rai's place. A narrow road and a large patch of land planted with gooseberry and lime that formed a part of his grounds lay between our houses, and a thin track led through it to the small blue gate that opened into his back garden. As my grandmother grew older, even that short distance became too much for her and she began to limit her walks to the driveway that led from one gate of our house to the other. And when that too became difficult for her, she would walk up and down on the front veranda.

My grandmother Shivrani Devi lived in the Godowlia house whenever she was in Banaras and not in Allahabad or in Lamahi, her husband Premchand's village. She could have lived with either of her two sons, both of whom were in Allahabad, but she preferred to live by herself. The house was too large for her, but it wasn't as if it was used by her alone. It was from where my father ran the Banaras branch of Saraswati Press, the publishing concern that had been set up by Premchand, and he'd rented the house for this purpose. It was a four-storeyed red building with long green doors and windows with louvres, the slats of which were stuck from lack of use, and in the afternoon the slanting sunlight filtering through them would create horizontal bars across the cracked cement floor. If you peered through the slats of the louvres in the room that housed the paper cutter, all you could see were little hills composed of the shreds that had been left over after the paper had been trimmed. The top floor was not in use, but the remaining three floors had balconies with wrought iron railings, from which you could look down into the central courtyard.

On most days there was a lot of activity on the ground floor. People would be seen arriving or leaving, there'd be the staccato sound of the printing machines, hand-carts piled high with bundles of books and paper would stop in the rather dark, musty lane that led off the main road on which the building stood, and the cargo would be loaded or unloaded. Right in front of the house was the Pandey Dharamshala and further down the road was Mazda Cinema. The second floor of the building had a marble floor and looked posher than the rest. This was where my father stayed when he was in town or put up his friends, artists or writers visiting Banaras. Away from the hubbub, my grandmother lived on the third floor with a goat and a servant called Pauwa. She'd send Pauwa to Ram Bhandar, the famous sweet shop, to get chumchums for us—pale orange, soaked in syrup, with sugar grains sticking to them—whenever we would visit her. It was Pauwa who would also bring supplies of atta, dal, rice, vegetables and other necessities.

The goat was tied in a little dark room at one end of the floor on which my grandmother lived. The small window in that room had a view of the street below. The goat would sometimes be seen at this window, looking out with expressionless eyes. Except at night, this road that was crowded with shops was busy at all hours. There'd be stray bulls and dogs, old rams with curving horns, rickshaws with seats sloping forward, cycles, hand-carts and people. The sky was dotted with paper kites. At regular intervals, funeral processions would pass by on the road in front of the house, and there'd be chants of *Ram nam satya hai!* The road eventually led to the Manikarnika burning ghat, which would ironically be bustling with life even as the biers of the dead, swathed in shrouds of white, pink, or yellow, were ferried along on it. Sometimes you could see a widow with shaven head, dressed in white, at the Pandey Dharamshala.

My grandmother too was a widow. In fact, she had been widowed twice, the first time when she was eleven years old. Her father Munshi Deviprasad had in 1905 written a treatise on the condition of Kayastha child widows. He had also put out an advertisement for the remarriage of his daughter. Premchand, who already had an early and unsuccessful marriage behind him, was a supporter of widow remarriage, and in order to practise what he preached, had decided that he'd only marry a child widow. He responded to the advertisement. His future father-in-law liked the response, and the marriage took place in 1906. When Premchand died in 1936, my grandmother became a widow for the second time, and she outlived him by forty years. They both believed in the ideals of Gandhi, and, in Premchand's phrase, were 'travellers on the same boat'. In the biography of her husband that she wrote in 1944, *Premchand Ghar Mein* (Premchand at Home), she mentioned that in February 1921 Premchand quit his government job soon after attending a meeting addressed by Gandhi in Gorakhpur. They returned to Lamahi where, in solidarity with Gandhi, they hired two carpenters to make charkhas which were then handed out free of cost in the village. In keeping with Gandhi's ideas and as a revolt against the fabrics imported from British mills, khadi was spun in homes across Lamahi. I always saw my grandmother wearing a white khadi sari with a thin border. Behind her gold-rimmed glasses her eyes had turned an oceanic grey due to cataract, and her homeopathic eye drops, *Cineraria maritima,* would be kept on the high windowsill of the room where she stayed when she visited us in Allahabad. She'd often ask one of us to put the drops in her eyes.

When I was eleven years old, the age at which she became a widow, I had no inkling about child marriage or the taboo on widows remarrying. It was only later, during a history lesson that I became aware of it, and realised that my grandmother too was one of those little girls who had been married and widowed even before they had figured out what matrimony was, and that according to the mores of the time, they were to remain widows for the rest of their lives. I'd never really thought of her in this light. She was simply our grandmother, a small woman who looked even smaller because she was bent with age. She'd arrive at Drummond Road a couple of times in the year from Banaras and always stayed in the hexagonal room with the high small windows in the front part of the house. It wasn't easy to think of that past of hers for it had been buried long ago. But she could hardly have been called a helpless widow who needed rescuing.

There were quite a few things about her that seemed to have nothing to do with who she was now. It was difficult to believe that she had once worked at the Lucknow-based Mahila Ashram and in 1929, under the influence of Gandhi, led a group of fifty-six women to a demonstration against cloth manufactured in Britain. Along with Premchand, she had also been arrested in Banaras for picketing against foreign cloth. She had given a rousing speech denouncing British rule at a public meeting of twelve thousand at the Mahila Ashram, and often been to jail. In fact, she thought that it was better for her to go to jail rather than her frail husband. She'd tell us about some of these things; even so, it was hard to conjure up a picture of that rather belligerent woman.

Instead, I see her sitting in the front veranda of our house on a charpoy the strings of which had become loose so that it sagged in the middle. She is trimming with a sharp pair of scissors the betel leaves that had just come in from the mandi. After she'd cut them all in the same size, she'd wrap them in a wet rag stained with *kattha* and put them away in a small wicker basket. She'd be annoyed if someone took a leaf or two from the basket because it upset her count. She was fastidious by nature and very precise in her habits. The little tin trunk that came with her from Banaras always held the same things, and when it was opened a particular smell emanated from it which I always associated with her. It was composed of the distinctive scent of kaker paan, of the camphor, which looked like small crumbly rocks, that she kept wrapped in paper, and of sitopaladi churna, the ayurvedic powder supposed to cure coughs, that she mixed with honey and licked off her index finger which was stained and marked with cuts from an old kitchen knife. When she came visiting, the rattling sound of the bamboos in the thicket near the Lamahi house seemed to enter with her, though it was not from Lamahi that she came but Banaras. She had a brother too, who had been five years old when she got married and whom she loved like a son. He was a political activist and once in a while he'd cycle all the way to Allahabad from Salempur, which she always called Sulempur, a distance of some 250 kilometres. He was tall and dark whereas she was small and fair; it was hard to believe that they were siblings.

While in Allahabad, she'd use all the three bathrooms in the house, each for the different rituals that formed her toilette. The land on which the house was built sloped gently down towards the gully that lay beyond the grounds. This meant that the bathroom at the furthest end of the house was situated at a lower level than the other two. She'd stand before the wash basin in this bathroom and endlessly scrub her hands. For the duration that she washed her hands, there'd be no water in the other bathrooms and led people to call out to her to close the bamba, the word that was used locally to mean the tap. During winter, water would be heated on a wood fire for her bath. The cauldron covered with a lid would turn sooty because of the smoke, and the steaming water would be placed in the bathroom designated by her for bathing. Her brass pot and the red bar of Lifebuoy that she used would be kept within reach on the window ledge that was made of red mosaic. She'd bathe, wrap the white khadi sari around her bird-like frame and go clattering back to her room in her khadauns. This was the sari that she'd washed a second time along with all the other clothes that had already been washed and ironed by the dhobi, for she couldn't get it out of her head that the dhobi scrubbed them with goat droppings. When she sat at the big dining table, her feet wouldn't reach the floor for she was small. There was a place on her thali fixed for each item of food, and when she was being served, she'd tap with her spoon in the designated spot, to make sure that the vegetable or the dal was in the right place. At breakfast she'd call out to us, to whichever of her grandchildren who happened to be passing by, break off a piece from her buttered roti and, with a trembling hand, she'd put it in our mouths. She found it difficult to eat without having fed someone else first.

Premchand Ghar Mein was not the only thing that Shivrani Devi wrote. Banarsidas Chaturvedi, a Hindi writer and journalist who knew Premchand, in his homage to the writer after his death, spoke of a statement Premchand had made in English and which Chaturvedi had translated for the tribute. In it, Premchand had refuted the charge that it was he who had written the stories that had appeared in his wife's name. He said that her stories were written in the rather brash voice of a *yoddhastree* or 'warrior woman', a voice that, given his mild nature, could not possibly have been his. Small and domineering, she is referred to elsewhere by Banarsidas Chaturvedi as 'Premchand's dictator'.

She was an astute woman with emphatic opinions and clear political leanings. Premchand depended on her to keep his life running smoothly so that he could write without having to bother with the niggling problems attendant on a provincial life. She participated in all that he did and, starting with their marriage which was a remarriage for both of them, they endorsed and were involved with some of the major reformist movements of the 1920s and 1930s. If the times shaped them, they too shaped the times; it was difficult to separate the personal from the political in their lives. Her biography of her husband is reverent, yet the voice of the 'warrior woman' is unmistakeable. While writing about his life, she was simultaneously inventing a rather strident past for herself—she made it very clear that she was not a woman who lived in purdah—and the image of her that emerges from the narrative is that of an educated woman, one used to reading and writing, a person with an independent mind.

The increased visibility of women in the public sphere in the 1930s affected literature as well. The writing of both men and women at the time dwelt on themes like female honour, modesty, sexual and moral purity, self-sacrifice, patriotism and motherhood. The women in Shivrani Devi's stories too are not quite free of all this. But she still had a slightly different notion of things. Her women know what they want and resolutely go about getting it. Again and again in her stories, women who have been robbed of all that they held dear are able to distance themselves from their sorrow, they are able to transcend the personal by including the village or the clan in their particular grief, or by devoting themselves to public service. In one of the stories, *Vidhvans ki Holi* (The Holi of Ruin), for example, the protagonist has lost all the members of her family to an earthquake, but there is no way she is going to succumb to the randomness of misfortune. In fact, she has to make up for her deprivation by being happier than she would have been, had the tragedy not taken place. She exhorts the villagers to celebrate Holi with her: 'The space fallen vacant in her heart was filled again in the auspicious flow of goodwill.'

One wonders if she would have written these stories of social reform and justice, had she not been Premchand's wife. In fact, would she have written at all? Early on in *Premchand Ghar Mein,* she admits that she had no interest in literature before her marriage and, in fact, had hardly been literate, something that is not surprising since she would then barely have been past the age of playing with dolls. What got her interested was *Soz-e-Vatan* (The Dirge of the Nation), published by Zamana Press in 1907, a year after she married Premchand. It was not Premchand's first work, though it was his first short story collection. He had already written the short novel *Asrar-e-Ma'abid* (The Secrets of God's Abode), which was serially published in 1903, and other novels including *Krishna* and *Prema*. But it was *Soz-e-Vatan* that piqued Shivrani's curiosity, for the book had stirred up quite a storm. Written in Urdu, a script that she could not read, it consisted of five patriotic stories that had been banned by the British for being seditious. A thousand copies of the book had been published, out of which three hundred had already been sold by the time it came to the notice of the government. James

Samuel Stevenson, the collector of Hamirpur district, where Premchand then lived, ordered a raid on his house. Shivrani tells us in *Premchand Ghar Mein* that the *Soz-e-Vatan* parcel had by then arrived from Kanpur, and they managed to retain one copy of the book. Around seven hundred copies were publicly burnt in the presence of Premchand. He was expressly forbidden to write anything without the permission of the District Collector.

What he did, then, was take a pseudonym, and Nawab Rai became Premchand. His reading aloud to Shivrani was not limited to *Soz-e-Vatan*. By now he was reading to her whatever he was writing at the time. And not just his own writing, he'd translate for her what he read in the English newspapers. It was for her, the beginning of a reading addiction—he'd read to her when he was home, and when he wasn't, she'd pick up the books herself. It was her initiation into the world of literature, and it wasn't long before she developed a desire to write her own stories. Often, she would write but tear up the stories without showing them to him. She didn't show him her first story, '*Saahas*' (Courage), that was published around 1913 in *Chand*. He came upon it on his own, and told her what a fool he'd felt when people at the *Chand* office laughed at the story and made fun of him. They suspected that he had written the story but ascribed it to her. It was with a mixture of embarrassment and irritation at what had happened that he asked her why she had suddenly become possessed by the demon of writing. It was, he said, an illness, and it was best that she did not bring this affliction upon herself. Yet he was pleased when she started showing him whatever she had written, and was even happier when her stories were translated into other languages. Much later, in 1937, a year after Premchand died, her stories were collected in a book, *Kaumudi*. It was published by Saraswati Press.

Being Premchand's wife must have put enormous pressure on Shivrani Devi. It not only influenced what she wrote but also who she *was*. If her stories had not existed, there would have been little chance of knowing the mind of this somewhat temperamental woman of whimsical habits. What kind of self-image did she have? Her biography of Premchand is strongly influenced by her point of view, and it is her dry, obliquely self-glorifying, rather audacious voice that is heard throughout. By presenting her own role in his life as the dominant one, she was carving out a radical past for herself. And while writing the stories of strong uncompromising women, we find her producing copies of herself, characters with the same sanctimonious 'moral' purpose and correctness. She writes these women in her self-image, but at the same time, while writing them she is also *becoming* like the women in her fiction. There is a constant give and take going on between the writer and her fictional creations. In the end, we cannot escape the feeling that Shivrani Devi's intransigent women bear an unsettling resemblance to her.

Many of the characters in her stories are, in fact, barely disguised representations of Self-Sacrifice, Honesty, Dignity, Justice, and Morality. They feel like cardboard cut-outs rather than real people. They quickly reveal the reason why they are in the story and are then forgotten. No more words are used than are absolutely necessary. The stories do not stray from the subject, just as she, in her own life, stuck to a well-defined trajectory with a sort of eccentric precision. She might have considered some details superfluous and either removed them from the stories or not written them at all, the very details that would have fleshed out the narrative. The reader who gets to the end of the rather skeletal stories might feel that they have just trekked across an arid landscape of the didactic. Shivrani often gets so carried away with her sense of purpose that, in order to demonstrate the moral, somewhat self-righteous idea behind the story, she resorts to the supernatural, to the melodramatic, and even to coincidence.

Of course, it wasn't just Premchand who was behind her ideas. It was also the times she was born in. Talking about all that she witnessed with her husband, she says in the preface to *Premchand Ghar Mein*: 'These are things that have taken place before my eyes. They are "his". He belonged to his readers, and so I present him to them. *I too do not belong to myself.*' She seems to think of herself as two people: one that is possessed by the 'higher duty' to society that she shared with her husband, and the other that looks at the humdrum, fallible and human part of her own self.

We can perhaps say that she too contributed to the triple erasure that was her destiny. To begin with, she was a woman, then she was a woman writer, and thirdly, she was Premchand's wife. In writing about Premchand, she obliterates herself, to the extent that we don't even know her date of birth or the details of her schooling or, except in passing, anything of her life before she married Premchand. Whatever we know about her is filtered through the prism of his life. And it has led to *Kaumudi* slipping into near oblivion. The book was not seen in the public domain for more than eighty years, until it was reissued in 2020, albeit with quite a few pages missing. She, along with other women writers, seemed to have a particular knack for disappearing.

In her last days, she complained that her mattress and the sheets on her bed were damp. It was December and the nights were cold. She was then living in a single room annexe that was located on one side of my uncle's garden. It was where she often chose to live when she was in Allahabad. We'd be sent to look in on her and we'd sit there fidgeting till we could escape into the fresh air outside. It was one of the things we knew about her, that she found it difficult to bear the cold. She'd never put on the fan even on scorching summer afternoons. Her way to beat the heat was simply to pace about restlessly. It was on one such afternoon that the clatter of her khadauns was heard. She came up to the bed on which I was sleeping and shook my shoulder. 'Are you asleep?' she asked rather unnecessarily. Of course, I was asleep, and she knew it. But seeing that I was now wide awake, with her typical contrariness she said, 'All right, go to sleep.'

The Invented Father

My father's name was Sripat Rai. His mother called him Dhunnu. This was because he was obsessive by nature, and if a particular *dhun* or whim took hold of him, he'd keep pursuing it till he had got what he wanted. But my mother didn't have a name for him at all. In her letters she addressed him as S. To us, he was Papa. He was a small man who occupied a large space in my world, a space too large if you kept in mind his slender physical form. He may have been about five feet five inches tall, inclining to slim, even thin. I eventually became almost as tall as he was, but he stayed taller than me for a long time. To see him I had to look up. My eyes always landed on his ears which stuck out from his head and tapered down to his jaw. He had no ear lobes. This made his ears look different from anyone else's. In fact, in most things he wasn't quite like anyone else I knew. Not that there were many I knew then. In his difference from other people lay the source of his mystery. But it was hard to pinpoint what that difference was.

You couldn't have called him handsome. There was nothing about him that would make him stand out in a crowd. To understand his face, you would have to know the changing climate of his moods. His nostrils would flare when he was pleased and a slight smile would play about his lips. When the smile reached his eyes, his face would open up like a book and you felt like you could read his thoughts. His limbs and his chest were quite hairless and a network of fine blue veins was visible through the fair skin of his arms and legs. But this wasn't why he was different. Perhaps it was the impression he gave of a suppressed energy which was about to break through, like the waters of a dammed up river.

He did not speak much, but I'd see him walking up and down the drive leading to the gate of our house, talking to himself, his hands moving in the air. He said little, but silence took up as much room as speech. I sought no explanation for his silence. It simply was, and I accepted it for what it was. Because he seldom spoke, I found myself thinking about him in pictures, though I did not immediately realise that I was thinking about him in images. His silence seemed to be coloured white, and to rest like snow on his shoulders. It was difficult to say why his shoulders looked as if they bore the weight of his silence. I thought, when I looked at them, of the ramparts of a castle, one that stood high on a hill and was impossible to penetrate. I'd never seen a castle, but I'd read about plenty of them. Above the castle, I imagined a heavy evening sky, its weight held in place by innumerable strings. Without the strings, the sky might have come crashing down.

My father seemed to be tied with invisible strings too, and fixed in one place; a quiet man, tethered to set habits. If it hadn't been for those strings he might have said something. He seemed always about to—something that might break the barrier of silence and make him accessible to the human realm, to my realm. A reassuring shower of words. When he did speak, it was softly, like a gentle murmur under the earth, and if your ears were not attuned to his pitch, you could easily miss what he said. They were just a few words, countable, insufficient, like pictorial puzzles. The bird that slept with its legs turned up in the air because it believed it was holding up the sky, the mile after mile of sand in the desert, with a mirage in the distance. Thirsty travellers could die chasing the mirage. M-i-r-a-g-e. He spelt out the word and explained what it meant. When it was very hot, you'd see a pool of water shimmering in the distance. It looked like water, but it was not water. It was an illusion created by the heat. There was an end-of-the-world feeling about these word-images. Cryptograms. What did they mean?

When he spoke to me, he'd use the masculine gender, as though I were a boy. This was not because he had wished for a son. He already had three sons and another daughter, my older sister. It was his particular form of expressing affection, though he could hardly be called a demonstrative man. Sometimes he'd catch hold of me and rub his cheek against mine. His two-day-old stubble would graze my skin and I'd struggle to free myself. He'd let me go then and laugh, the loud and infectious laughter that he had inherited from his father, and that set his eyes twinkling. That was still the time when my interactions with him were not without a measure of pain; one way or the other, it was the pain of inaccessibility, or the pain of contact. It took me a long time to realise that if I was shy of him, he was shy of me. The distance between us seemed unbridgeable. Whatever he said to me, his youngest, seemed to have no meaning, or not a meaning that I could relate to. It was all banter and teasing, an elusive register of speech.

Sitting at the big dining table, we'd eat our meals in silence. If my mother passed a dish to him, he'd always refuse it with a frown, but pick up the same dish later. This mortified me. I understood only later that he did this because he did not like to be noticed. He was a self-conscious man. But my mother, always attentive to him, noticed each thing that he had, or did not have on his plate, and looked hurt when he refused what she offered. He'd insist that we eat whatever had been cooked without making a fuss, if, for instance, one of us didn't want to eat the bitter gourds or the turnips that were on the menu. If you were sitting next to him, he'd serve you a good helping of the wholesome item that usually tasted awful. He'd insist on salad. At such times, we thought of him as a tyrant. Yet mealtimes were not unpleasant. The silence at the table was broken only by the sound of spoons clinking inside steel katoris or against the plates as we ate our turnip curry, and in the silence, you could hear the companionable sound of the family chewing. The golden rule of silence was broken one day when my father suddenly whistled in the middle of the meal. We'd eat our rice and dal with our fingers, and it was when he was slurping the mix into his mouth that we heard with his indrawn breath, the involuntary whistle. He continued to eat without saying a thing, as if whistling while sitting at the table was something that he did every day. He was always telling us not to whistle.

Once when I was about five years old, I ran away from home. I had no particular reason for doing so and there was no plan in my head. It wasn't as if I was escaping from anything. My life at home could not have been more comfortable. It was more likely that I did not recognise boundaries then, did not understand that there were limits beyond which I could not go. The compound was large, so it may have been easy just to keep going, boundary wall and gate notwithstanding—just a little geographical confusion. I remember roads lined with trees, tamarind, I now know. It must have been the tamarind-lined Thornhill Road, not far from Drummond Road. What I remembered afterwards was not the running away but the coming back. As it happened, there was a rickshaw driver who recognised me and brought me home. The walk up the curving drive of the bungalow seemed endless, with the man firmly clasping my arm lest I run away again. My father stood on the veranda, which was a couple of feet higher than ground level. From where I stood, with the two extra feet of the veranda added to his height, he seemed very tall. He could have asked me where I had gone. What he did ask, in his subterranean voice, was *why* I had gone. I never forgot the question. It kept returning to me, seeming to query what lies at the root of anything we do. There never is an adequate answer.

But before the real father, there was the father that I had invented. I created him out of the scraps of information that I had about him, the father whom I had never met. The man as he was before I was born. There were the words written by his mother, a passing mention of the son in her biography of her husband, *Premchand Ghar Mein*—her son, my father, who was a child then. Was he a baby once? It was hard to imagine him as one. An angry infant, the mother wrote. When he is given milk in a feeding bottle, he bites off the rubber nipple in rage. In my mind, a child attached itself to a milk bottle, small, furious—possessed both of teeth and of temper. Too young then, but he was soon to start walking.

On a bright day, with the sun coming in from the slatted window of his father's writing room in Gorakhpur where he was posted as Deputy Inspector of Schools, the four-year-old child wandered in. There was an article, recently finished by his father, waiting on the table to be sent off for publication. It was 1921, soon after Premchand, mesmerised by Gandhi at his meeting in Gorakhpur on 8 February, had resigned from his government job and joined the Non-cooperation Movement. Without a regular income coming in, the family subsisted mainly on the money that came in from Premchand's writing. The child went up to the article, tore it up, took another sheet and began to write on it himself. Later, when a horrified Premchand discovered the shreds of an article that was to be sent off the same day, the normally mild-mannered man slapped his son.

The next thing I knew about him was from his own account of how he had started school. I thought of the eight-year-old boy walking on the dusty road that led from Lamahi, his father's village, to Pandeypur, a suburb of Banaras where the primary school was located. He was going to get himself admitted to the school. There were mahua and mango trees on both sides of the road, but they soon thinned out. The sun was blinding, the boy was barefoot, and from his shoulder hung a sling bag which contained three items: a black writing slate, a stick of khadiya or white chalk and a small pouch containing a lump of jaggery and some sattu, the nutritious flour made from gram and barley that his mother had thoughtfully packed for him. She did not know that he could, like a camel, go without food for hours. That proclivity he displayed only years later. The boy's eyes were set on the road ahead. There was no shade. The school was nowhere in sight and he was tired by the time he reached it.

There was a small room with a desk. The wall behind the desk was a vivid blue. There was a man sitting at the desk. The school master, for that was who the man was, pushed back his glasses and asked the boy the name of his father. Dhanpat Rai, said the boy. The master then asked him for his date of birth. The boy did not know his date of birth. His mother had never told him. And to get this piece of information, suddenly so vital, he would have to go back to ask her. He thought of the long way he had just walked. He could not possibly go back all that way again. Then he had a brainwave. He remembered his mother telling him he was born in the rains. His mind made a quick calculation; he rooted about for a date and succeeded in conjuring one out of nowhere: 16 July 1916. And so, he was born into the world. He now had an official identity. The date stayed with him for the rest of his life.

In the autumn of 1994, three months after he died, in my mind, my father the schoolboy, quite suddenly became an adult. Sitting on the red terrazzo floor of the room in which he had died, I looked through the neatly stacked copies of *Studio International* in the bottom shelf of his Godrej cupboard. The cupboard was mostly bare, but in the shelf above the one which held *Studio*, pressed under a large illustrated book on Auschwitz, *We Shall Not Forget*, I found a makeshift file, which consisted of two separate sheets of cardboard tied together with string. There were photographs inside that had been marked and perhaps set aside for publication. One of them showed Premchand on his death bed, the tendons in his neck standing out, a shadowy beard, his hair still dark and the eyebrows like black wings. His eyes looked straight at the camera as if to ask, what has it all been about? In another photo, he was dead. He had his face turned away from the camera; the eyes were closed. The bier was on the floor. My eyes travelled not to the dead man but to the one beside him—my father, who was twenty years old when his father died.

8 October 1936, the day on which Premchand died, a Thursday, would have been like any other day in Banaras. The rains would be over by then, but the city must still have exhaled the muggy heat of a rainy season. There would have been garlands of marigold draped on the shroud, rose and jasmine petals showered on the bier, a smell of faded blooms on the air. My father, never comfortable in the midst of people, would have worried about what he should do. He must have wandered around, bumping into people, feeling watched as he did so. What was expected of him? Was there a pattern of

behaviour that he must conform to? Some death ritual that he was expected to know—a code of mourning that the sons of dead fathers must adhere to? He didn't have a clue about any of this. Knowing in later years what I did of him, I thought his predominant emotion must have been one of embarrassment at suddenly feeling so naked, his emotions on display, as it were. A crowd of mourners had gathered for the much-loved writer who had so much writing still left in him. The young man would have walked up with an impassive face and taken hold of one end of the bamboo frame that made up the bier, stepped out into the street at the head of the throng of people as it walked past Ramkatora Park, chanting *Ram Nam Satya Hai* on its way to the Manikarnika cremation ghat by the Ganges.

I could see him at night after he came back from the funeral knowing that his father's account with life had been settled. He must have thought about the responsibilities he had inherited; the books that must continue to be published, for his father had devoted his life to writing them. He already had a BA degree from Allahabad and decided to study no further; his brother Amrit, now fifteen years old, had to finish his education, and he had a mother to look after. There were debts to be paid off. He must have lain awake for much of the night. I thought about him and the shadows began to move.

He'd go to Saraswati Press every day. Even though he was not away from home for long, his departure was not without ceremony. He'd start the silver-grey Studebaker Commander that he drove at the time, accelerating the stationary car that stood in the portico till it sounded like a plane ready to take off, with the rush of air from the exhaust pipe setting the leaves on the driveway fluttering madly. The Allahabad branch of

Saraswati Press was in Civil Lines. It was a set of three rooms on the first floor at one end of a long veranda. Beside the entrance, there was a stool on which sat the peon whose right hand was missing the index finger. The spacious main room of the set was almost circular, with large wire-meshed windows that looked down onto the crossing of Sardar Patel Road and Mahatma Gandhi Marg. But you could hardly see anything through them because they were never cleaned and, as a result, let in little light. There were books arranged on open shelves that reached up to the roof; most of them were multiple copies of Premchand titles, some of other Hindi writers that included the whole set of Agyeya's works, and quite a lot of literature from other countries that my father had got translated and published. He was fond of the Tolstoy story 'How Much Land Does a Man Need?' He'd talk about the six feet of land that lay waiting at the end of a human life.

It was high summer. The *loo* blew all day, colouring the air yellow and blowing dust in people's eyes. Suddenly the roadsides and vegetable markets were full of melons and watermelons. They were supposed to be the sweetest when the heat was at its peak. The melons were yellow, with dark green stripes running the length of the fruit, like longitude lines on a diagram of the earth. They smelt delicious, with a flavour that got absorbed by the milk and other consumables with which they shared space in the fridge. They also smelt of the riverbed where they were cultivated. My mother asked me to slice and bring to the table one of the melons to be served as dessert. I remember cutting the melon horizontally into half, then into thick unpeeled slices, all in a matter of five minutes. My silent father glanced at the fruit on the plate and, quite suddenly, he was furious. He spoke. Had I not taken a good look at the melon? Seen the way the stripes on it ran? If I had not, then didn't I have eyes, and if I did, then why had I cut the fruit crosswise? After all, nature had drawn the lines on the fruit for a reason, that it should be cut the right way. There was room for argument here, but there was no way I could have argued with him. And something struck me just then. I suddenly saw the melon not as something to be simply eaten, but as a living thing with an aesthetic of its own. It was the first time I saw a melon, even though I had been looking at melons for as long as I could remember.

Summer evenings in Allahabad hang heavy. The air turns still, not a leaf stirs. Night falls with uncanny suddenness, increasing the size of the leaves on trees. People emerge from inside their homes and stand about in listless groups, talking desultorily, affected by that strange mix of restlessness and desolation that seems to fall from the sky. The shops close early; there are not many places to go and not many people who drop by for a visit. From the dark, the cicadas set up their incessant high chirruping. It seems to merge with the humming of the blood, a pervasive cascading sound that draws you into its hypnotic rhythm. The mosquitoes will come later, with the rains. As will the flying termites and the moths that shed their papery wings in rustling heaps under the lights to which they are compulsively drawn, fluttering to their death.

Once in a while, to relieve the evening monotony, Papa would take us out for ice-cream to Kwality or to Guzder's. Before we could be taken out, certain conditions had to be met. We had to go wash our face and hands, put on shoes and socks. The two things were connected in some fundamental way; if your face and hands were washed, you had to be wearing shoes and socks too. It is a little puzzling to me now, the shoes and socks rule. Allahabad is hot for eight months of the year. Shouldn't open sandals have been the footwear of choice? I don't know who was responsible for this particular detail of the family dress code. Or was it just something that was common to everyone in the middle class? All middle class children wore shoes and socks, at least when they appeared in society. It could have been that my mother, who had an urban aristocratic Shia Muslim background, had fallen in with the prevalent taste for things colonial. My father belonged to Lamahi, where shoes could not have been a compulsory item of dress. In fact, he may have spent his childhood clambering up and down trees, wading in the village pond, or walking about quite shoeless. But that may in turn have triggered a hankering for shoes.

There was some fuss around shoes in the home of my childhood, largely to do with my father's insistence on cultivating habits of thrift in us. We were not bought new shoes till we could prove that the old ones were battered beyond repair. Once the shoes had been proven to be no longer usable, a trip to Civil Lines became necessary. We climbed into the back of the Studebaker, resting our heads against the seats, curious about the way our hair stuck and unstuck on the nylon covers with a thin crackling sound. We headed to Kapoor and Sons, dealers in shoes, handbags and other leather goods. Suitable black leather shoes with lace fasteners and crepe soles were bought for the boys and a variation on the same, with a strap across the front for the girls. It was always the same boring shoes, utility rather than style being the guiding principle.

There was some 'shoe-talk' always floating around the house. About the villager who slept on a bench in a park when he came to the city, keeping his shoes under his head; they served as a pillow and were at the same time saved from getting stolen. Or about a cousin's handmade leather sandals that had come all the way from Peshawar. We had a relationship with shoes. Either they shrank and became too small so that they needed to be stretched on a cobbler's mould to increase the size, or they became hard and had to be soaked in oil to soften them up. Cherry Blossom Boot Polish was bought in large quantities and stocked in the old cupboard at one end of the gallery. It was fascinating to watch Shankar, the helper who did odd jobs around the house, line up the shoes to be polished. He'd open the rectangular box, inside which were the small, round, flat jars of black-, brown- or cherry-coloured boot polish, hog hair brushes and a stained rag that was used to give the final flourish to the shoes after they were done. A sharp smell of turpentine mixed with lanolin rose when the tins of Cherry Blossom were opened. They transformed the shoes from dull, dusty, and pedestrian items of daily use to sparkling, flashing things lit with a myriad lights that seemed to emanate from them. It was as if the very soul of the shoes had come alive.

At the end of my parents' first visit to Europe in 1960, they brought back from Holland a pair of child-sized shoes made entirely of chocolate, a replica of the shoes in Van Gogh's painting. The mouth-watering shoes in their transparent case sat in the glass-fronted cupboard for months, no one having the heart to eat them, till summer melted them into a brown gooey mess that could finally be consumed. There were other stories from that European trip that were repeated so often in the family that they became legends. The one about the silent walk, for instance. My father decided to see Paris on foot. I don't know if my mother was consulted on this, but she found herself trudging along behind him as he walked on and on without a word, covering at a regular pace the famous landmarks, the Champs-Élysées, the Eiffel Tower and Trocadéro, the Jardin du Luxembourg, the Panthéon and Saint-Michel. It didn't end there. There were also the museums: the Musée d'Orsay, the Orangerie and the Jeu de Paume. They walked from one museum to the other not only without speech, but also without food. My father was able to make do without food for hours; not so, my mother. At one point, when she said she was hungry, a baguette was bought. It was more than a foot long, was crisp and smelt delicious. However, feeling embarrassed to eat a bread of such conspicuous size all the while walking, she at last succeeded in placing the baguette, too large for it, into the hat held out by a beggar who fortuitously appeared out of nowhere.

A certain pride was taken in the idea of being poor in our quite well-to-do household. There was the unspoken belief that being poor was somehow spiritually exalting. This had something to do with the ideals of my grandfather that were imbibed by the next generation, including my father. Premchand had led the frugal life of a penurious school teacher, rising at odd hours of the night or early morning to write what became the many volumes of his fiction, often only by the light of a hurricane lamp. His commitment to the poor and the downtrodden was well known, as was his belief that money corrupts. This distaste for money, or rather the idea of money, was transmitted to his progeny, and by a complex process of genetic osmosis, to the next generation as well. I remember saying, in response to a polite question by a visitor as to what I would like to be when I grew up, that I would like to be poor.

My father's relationship with money was complex. Along with a certain earthy thriftiness, which could have been dictated by an aesthetic aversion to excess, he was also prone to bouts of extreme generosity. He would gift someone money towards buying a house, an air-conditioner, a bed, a book, a car, anything really, that was needed by someone he was fond of, their place in his affections being a key requirement. Not a soul knew about what he gave away. Later, after he died, someone said of him that 'his left hand did not know what the right gave away'. When I think about my father and his relationship with money, the air around him seems to grow thick with contradictions. Having no expensive tastes or extravagant habits, he had no use for money. Yet he made a lot of money in his lifetime, mainly through publishing the books of his father and of other prominent writers. At one point, Saraswati Press had offices in Banaras, Allahabad, Lucknow, Delhi, Patna and a couple of other cities. It was a small publishing empire that he had built up from scratch.

Characteristically inscrutable, my father had once, in a mix of pride, disgust and bitter disparagement of himself, said that he had made enough money 'to last for seven generations'. Yet when he returned to Allahabad towards the end of his life, stricken by a mysterious malaise of which there was no physical evidence, it was with little money. No one really found out what happened to his wealth, but then his money-world had always existed in a secluded zone, with none privy to its ups and downs. He seemed to have something on his mind, and in his last days had become a Dostoyevsky-like figure haunted by thoughts that gave him no peace.

It is in the 1970s. When my mother or one of us asks him for money, a frown creases his forehead. He asks about the amount involved. He always asks. It is necessary for him to ask, for how can he give the money when he doesn't know how much? But it makes us squirm. Then he counts each rustling note, making sure that no two notes are stuck together, rubbing them between his thumb and forefinger till the paper crackles. We take the notes and hurry out of the mahogany door with its swirling grains embedded deep in the wood, shutting it softly, very carefully, so as not to seem in indecent haste. But there was more to the money story. In a baffling ambiguity quite cancelling out the counting of the notes, his wallet would lie carelessly in his unlocked cupboard, within easy reach, and the tacit understanding was that anyone of us who needed money could help ourselves to it from his wallet. We often did. No explanations were ever asked or given.

Many years later, when I was living in Australia, new to the country and with few resources, I was working at various jobs, trying to make ends meet. On a banksia-scented morning, with the wattle in full bloom and the wind sighing through the gum trees, I remember a letter arriving from India. My name and address were on the envelope in his beautiful, flowery handwriting. I slit it open and found inside a single narrow rectangular note, green in colour. A hundred US dollars. It had come not by registered but ordinary post, to reach me or not, the decision already out of his hands, left as it were to fate. There was nothing else in the envelope, no letter to explain what the money was for, or how he happened to have US dollars. He had always been a man of few words.

I try to make sense of my father's paradoxical attitude to money; to juxtapose the energy it must have taken to put together a wealth that while not enormous, was substantial enough for us to lead a comfortable life, and what amounted to an instinctive revulsion for money, the very thing that made that life possible. I remember a dark winter night. It was quite late; it may have been around ten at night, though it felt like later. The normal activities of the house had wound down. I remember fireflies glowing in the dark outside the veranda, but this is a false memory. There could have been no fireflies, for they came only in the rains. It was a moonlit night.

The doors of the house were closed against the cold, but a voice had been heard. Someone had called out. Then there was a sound of knocking or tapping—wood on wood. Screened from view, I looked out of the glass door of the drawing room.

There seemed to be an indistinct, shapeless mass on one of the cane chairs, which, aquamarine in the daytime, seemed to have absorbed the darkness of the man sitting on it and looked quite black. For the mass had by then resolved itself into a distinct head, attached to a body swathed in blankets, sitting leaning a little forward, silhouetted in the faint yellow light spreading thinly from the single forty-watt yellow bulb at the other end of the veranda. There was a thick bamboo stick leaning against a chair. This is what he must have knocked with, making the sound I had heard.

He had by now been recognised, and there was a flurry of activity inside the house. The iron bolt was shot back, the door creaked open and my father went out to meet the man. There was a conversation in low tones, which went on for maybe ten minutes. I don't remember what happened after that, but maybe he was asked to stay the night. The next morning is a blank. There was some conversation around that night-time visitor. Apparently, he was the son of a well-known industrialist who had decided to renounce the family wealth. I don't know how he knew my father, but he had stopped by to meet him. My mother commented on the odd hour he had chosen. He was on his way to the Himalayas on foot. To meditate and introspect. I wonder what my father made of the mysterious caller and whether he thought about him later in life, when he started giving away his own things in an obscure act of renunciation, till he was left with little of his not inconsiderable possessions.

I never found out the name of the visitor and never thought of asking my father.

Lightfastness

It may be that a better way
To conquer time and world
Is to pass and not to leave a trace—
To pass, and not to leave a shadow
On the walls …
It may be that the better art
Is with the hand of Bach
To leave the organ undisturbed—
To vanish, not to leave a cinder
For the urn … to be, but by deceit:
To strike yourself from latitudes
To slip through time as through the sea
And not to break the waves

—Marina Tsvetayeva, 14 May 1923

The square, orange boxes made of cardboard had been shipped all the way from England. They contained the Winsor and Newton tubes of paint that my father used in the decades when he was painting oils, and they remained lying around the house for many years after he died. Some of the boxes had never been opened. The viscous oil colours dried up and hardened, and the tight caps were difficult to unscrew. Raw Umber, Gamboge, Cobalt Blue, Scarlet Lake, Ultramarine, Purple Lake, Rose

Madder, Umber Hue, Russet, Chrome Yellow, Cerulean Blue, Sap Green, Viridian Green, Cadmium Yellow, Burnt Sienna.

My father Sripat Rai started painting relatively late in life, when he was already past forty. The inspiration to paint must have come, I thought, from my mother who was, at the time, painting floral patterns on clay vases. He'd sit there, quietly watching her. Then one day, he quite suddenly took to making pastel drawings in a sketch book, and moved quickly to doing studies of flowers in pastels, which were later framed and hung in the house in sets of twos and threes. Sometimes he'd get interested in the 'drawing' homework that we got from school and help us colour in the simple forms. In fact, when asked in an interview about when and how he started painting, he said, 'It was my children. One day I picked up their watercolours and, with them, started daubing. I have not stopped.' Soon he was painting with a passion, experimenting with colour and form, using brush, spatula and knife. He'd sometimes set up an easel outside where the light was better and later move to his studio inside.

He was gradually moving in the direction where scenic representation mutated into abstract form. He painted shades of the main colour as receding or advancing planes, with a few recognisable forms—spires, triangles and rectangles—built into the landscape. One of his paintings was titled *The Bridgehead*, another, *Church in the Far Distance*. He frequently used shades of white or a range of the same spectrum of colours, for instance violet-indigo-blue-green, which gave the paintings a shimmering feel. Even in paintings with titles like *Advent of Spring* or *Out in the Sun*, he was not depicting a scene, nor was he trying to represent an experience that he had gone through. In the fumbling with form and colour, he was seeking a pictorial language that could best express emotion. One of his paintings, *Flowering Sadness*, was an asymmetrical arrangement of rectangular or hexagonal shapes done in orange, brown, mauve, blue and white. In landscapes, there was the possibility of mixing the abstract with the figurative, and it was this possibility, I felt, that must have led him to paint them.

You could sense his awareness of the seasons in the landscapes. He'd talk of the six seasons in this part of the world and he'd speak aloud their sonorous names—Vasanta, Grishma, Varsha, Sharad, Hemanta and Shishira. They seemed to encompass the turning of the earth and the regenerating processes of nature in a way that set them apart from the four seasons of spring, summer, autumn and winter.

He'd paint furiously, and in no time, there were a lot of paintings. They were stacked against the walls of the room, which looked out onto the driveway, that he used as his studio, and they hung on the walls in every room of our house. They were put up in the gallery that ran the breadth of the house, separating the front rooms from those at the back. A diffuse light filtered in from the skylights situated high in the gallery and glanced off the walls, settling on the paintings and simultaneously absorbing and reflecting the colours. The Winsor and Newton rolls of canvas that he used, also dispatched from London, were large. He'd cut them to the size he wanted with a pair of big sharp scissors, then stretch them out onto a frame that he put together using a hammer and nails from the pinewood that had already been prepared by a carpenter.

There was an old clock in its teak case on the pistachio-green wall of the room adjoining his bedroom. The dial was in Roman numerals and was visible through the glass face. Below this glass face was another round glass through which you could see the golden pendulum. The clock would chime at the quarter, half and full hour, the longest and most rapturous at the full. It was a mechanical clock, manufactured in England, with its make—Enfield Eastern Clock—written on the dial. My father would wind it once a week with an ornate key of fine workmanship. It was always on the same day of the week, for he was a man of set habits. The chiming of the clock kept pace with our childhood and also with the years in Allahabad when my father was painting. He'd start mid-morning, lean the canvas up against the wall, and squatting on a bed-sized piece of plywood in a pungent cloud of linseed and turpentine oils, he'd get to work with the knife or spatula. He'd break for lunch and then be back at work, carrying on till late afternoon, for as long as the light lasted. This was on Sundays, for on weekdays, he'd go to Saraswati Press, to deal with his publishing business. He was Premchand's elder son and had inherited the responsibility of publishing his father's works, of seeing to it that the books never went out of print. 'I have worked at it ceaselessly,' he said in an interview, 'bringing out editions of my father's works, recently as much as eighteen hours in the day.' But this meant that he found little time for painting, and as a result, he got the reputation of being a Sunday painter. He never went to an art school and was firmly of the opinion that art was not something that could be taught. Either you had it in you, or you didn't.

It was not long before he began to feel a little isolated in Allahabad where there were no other painters and no art scene to speak of. Looking for the stimulus of a big city and a peer group of artists, he slowly began, in the early sixties, to spend more time in Delhi, living first in rented accommodation till he bought his own house in Hauz Khas in the late sixties and shifted to Delhi on a permanent basis. R/7 Hauz Khas Enclave stayed his address for almost two decades. He kept an open house where Ramchander the cook, wearing a self-styled cap with the peak turned at an angle to hide his bald pate, was ready each evening with a meal enough for a dozen people, even though my father lived alone in Delhi at the time. And visitors did drop by every evening, especially towards the end of the month when impoverished young poets, writers and journalists, their money having run out, would come to R/7 confident of being able to get whisky and dinner.

He set up a work corner in the new house, here too with a bed-sized piece of plywood pushed up against the wall, on which he rested the canvas he was currently working on. With clear vital eyes in his lean face and an air of spruce energy, he'd sit crouching barefoot on the plywood, with open tubes of paint, a palette and bottles of linseed and turpentine oil beside him. He'd started painting rather large canvases by then, believing that it was not as much what he painted but how it was done, the clarity of seeing, that mattered. It was at this time that he appeared to gather himself in his paintings, to create and to be immersed in them. The paintings did not mirror the world with its known objects, but rather they seemed to be the sensual play of a temperament that was essentially quiet.

But he'd never been an easy man to understand. After having spent two decades on art, when things seemed to be going well for him—he exhibited, in 1963, twenty-four landscapes at the Kunika-Chemould Gallery, and the same year, two of his paintings were sent to the Seventh Tokyo Biennale—he decided to give up painting. The reasons for this relinquishing of something that had been a passion were never clear. Thereafter, he'd sit, staring into space for hours, on the battered sofa that had been brought from Allahabad and was now in the upstairs living room of R/7. The colour of the old sofa was a faded olive green, and it seemed to repeat the hue of the dusty trees outside.

The grey stuffing showed through the threadbare cloth and the sofa, with the springs having lost their elasticity, had sunk in the middle, adapting to the shape of my father's body. He always sat on the same sofa, one of a set of three, placed at an awry angle that caused unease in those with an instinct for straightness. There was a definitiveness about the awkward angle; a finality that declared itself at first glance and could not be interfered with. If he entered the room and noticed that the angle had been even slightly altered, maybe during a round of cleaning in his absence, he'd frown and immediately change it back again, as if his well-being was somehow poised on the exactness of that angle. The sofa was drawn up right next to a tall standard lamp, visible as soon as you entered the room. It had lost the shade it came with, and so, a naked bulb shone brightly atop it in the evenings.

This was a time when the day would go by and he'd be sitting there in the unlit room doing nothing at all. Now and then he'd open a cylindrical, black plastic box with John Player Special written on it in gold letters, and a monogram composed of the letters J, P, and S complicatedly intertwined. My father would draw from it a Chancellor cigarette that was chocolate in colour, with two golden lines circling the filter which he'd then light carefully, his cupped hand shading the flame from the match, his face suddenly illuminated. There was an empty cardboard carton of Aristocrat Whisky placed close to the sofa, into which he'd drop the ash. There were several windows in that large room which might have opened onto the murky, white Delhi sky, but he never did open them. The windows with frosted glass panes were bare, and once when my mother tried to put up curtains, he told her he didn't like curtains. There was nothing hidden in his life, he said. Curtains meant secrets. Nevertheless, he spoke little and told no one of what went on in his head, or indeed in his life, and this gave him an aura of secretiveness.

There was the time when two reporters and a cameraman arrived from Doordarshan TV to interview the painter-publisher elder son of Premchand. My father's response to this invasion of his privacy was to pick up a newspaper and, legs folded beneath him on the sofa, disappear behind it till the intruders had gone away. This was quite in keeping with his unpredictable nature; he could be aloof to the point of rudeness. Sometimes he looked as if he wanted to say something, but he said nothing. Perhaps he was waiting. What did he wait for? Heat shimmered on the opaque glass panes of the empty windows, and the changing light outside would turn them into rosy panels in the early morning, a seething white at mid-day, deep purple in the evening and black at night. He'd then switch on the lights.

One day three delivery men carried a radiogram into the upstairs living room where he spent most of his time. He'd bought it from Rhythm Corner in South Extension. The deep chestnut-coloured wood of the radiogram had been polished to a glossy piano finish. The lower half of the cabinet was fronted with transparent blue glass and set with a mirror at the base that seemed to magnify the space inside. It held a record player, a radio, and a Grundig spool tape recorder. The lid slid in smoothly at even a slight touch and the door of the cabinet swung down to reveal the three devices, safe inside from dust and damp. Late into the evening, my father would listen, engrossed, to Rabindra Sangeet by Pankaj Mullick, Kanika Bandhopadhyay, Arghya Sen and Sumitra Sen, whose records he had bought from a shop in Bengali Market. He'd listen to Bengali folk singers, Lalan Fakir, Purnadas Baul, Atul Prasad and Rajanikanta Sen. Dressed in a white dhoti with a thin black border, he'd sit on the faded green sofa with his legs drawn up under him, beating time with one hand on the curved wooden arm-rest of the sofa, though his rhythm did not at all match that of the song. Could it be that the immediacy and the solitude of music gave him the creative inspiration that he sought? But he had already stopped painting by this time.

Once or twice every month, he would go to the British Council Library, which was at the time located on Rafi Marg, in the same building as the All India Fine Arts and Crafts Society, and return with an armload of books. He liked reading biographies and literary criticism. You were allowed to borrow six books at a time from BCL. Once in a while, I went to the library with him. I remember inhaling the smell of the books and coming away with a vague feeling, familiar to me from my early childhood, that the exercise of reading was olfactory rather than visual. If I found something I wanted to borrow he didn't mind his quota of six being cut down to four or five. He was keen that we should read, and when I was ten, my sister and I received from him *The Adventures of Galldora* by Modwena Sedgwick. He had brought the book for us from Delhi, and it had 'For Seema and Sara' inscribed on the fly-leaf, with 'Papa' squeezed in beside them. The date was 5 December 1966. The book was about a rag doll called Galldora and was meant for younger readers, but Galldora's name was an anagram for who she was. It was a discovery that there could be a word hidden inside another word, with a meaning apart from the obvious one.

In the few conversations I had with him about painting, he told me about some of the materials and techniques that went into the making of a painting. What gouache or body colour was, and how it could be used to achieve an effect of opacity on a finished painting, or about tempera, which is permanent and fast drying, made up of pigments mixed with a water-soluble binder such as egg yolk. He spoke of the Florentine painters of the Renaissance—Botticelli, Caravaggio, Raphael and Titian, who had used egg tempera for their paintings, probably because of the long-lasting nature of the medium. While talking of other painters, he hinted that his own preference was for impasto in which undiluted paint is applied with a palette knife so thickly on the canvas that it stands out above the surface of the painting, causing light to be reflected in new ways. It could be used to convey a broken, textured quality of light. Raw Umber, he said, was a natural brown or reddish-brown earth pigment that he often used, and the name came from the Latin word *umbra*, which meant shadow. With dusk falling outside the window and muting colours, he told me about lightfastness. This was the property that determined how resistant a pigment was to fading; some colours were transient and faded within a few months, while others had greater permanence.

Many years later, when he was no longer around, I thought about lightfastness, wondering if something like it adhered to human lives as well. Some lives faded away while others survived in public memory. Through the journal *Kahani*, which my father edited from 1954 to 1979—where the early fictions of Phanishwarnath Renu, Ram Kumar, Nirmal Verma, Krishna Sobti, Mohan Rakesh, Agyeya, and Bhisham Sahni among others first appeared—and the books that he published from Saraswati Press, he shaped the sensibility of a whole generation of readers and writers. There was also the house he rented on 14 Hastings Road in Allahabad in the 1940s, which functioned as a writers' commune, and under its umbrella was published *Prateek*, the influential journal that heralded modernism in Hindi. It was also the address from where Agyeya edited the *Saptak* anthology series of poetry. Despite all of the work that my father did to promote modernism in Hindi letters, which included the regular translation and publication in Hindi of foreign literatures—European, British, Russian, South African and Chinese—along with those from other Indian languages, he was forgotten almost immediately after his death. The editorials that he wrote for *Kahani* were collected while he was still alive in *Kahani ki Baat,* but the book soon went out of print and has never been reprinted.

He was a man of nomadic creative impulses. Off and on, he translated from Hindi. He wrote a few stories in Hindi too, under the pen name Akalank Mehta. I did not know about the stories till after he died. I read a couple of them in the memorial issue of *Kahani* that was published after his death by my brother in an attempt to revive the magazine. Even so, it was painting that he was obsessed with. The canvasses that he left behind, the ones that were finished and those that lay rolled up and incomplete spilled into all the empty spaces of our house. They should have been the lasting testimony to a life. Yet, he escaped the paintings as he did much else. When I tried to think about him, all I could come up with were a few images and even fewer words. He remained shadowy in substance; each effort to understand him threw up an elusive lack of palpability, a feeling that even after having lived so close to him, in death he had clean got away from us all. His life, the little that I knew of it, was now fiction, and I could make of it what I would.

He died on 9 July 1994, exactly a week before he turned seventy-eight. It had been a day of intermittent rain; short sharp showers alternating with dazzling sunshine. Clouds trailed across the sky. The neem tree outside the window of the room where he lay was large and still, casting oppressive shadows. The sharp smell of neem berries hung in the air. He had been lying like that for the last four days, ever since he had a stroke that paralyzed the left side of his body, unable to speak, any movement difficult, refusing to eat, looking about him with his eyes wide open. He seemed to hover between two worlds as if in two minds—unable to leave, unable to stay.

Death had been something of an obsession with him. 'Look,' he'd said, holding out his hand in front of him, when he was in relatively good health. 'My hand is so steady, how will I die?' And now, on one of those last anxious mornings while he was still able to speak, he asked. 'If you don't eat, how long will it take for life to cease?' How long can a human being last without food? His hair had grown long. Always clean-shaven, he now had a stubbly beard. His nails, yellow, had not been cut in a while. He did not recognise the few visitors who dropped by to see him and sat there looking as if he'd seen a ghost. He'd developed a reluctance to live, and in his last illness, resisted all attempts made by us at medical intervention. He'd been a self-willed man. Here, too, he made a clear choice. It was death above life.

It was a moment he had been preparing for. His own father, Premchand, had died at the age of fifty-six. He'd expected to go the way of his father. Fifty-six. Each year he lived beyond that was an add-on. He'd started giving away his things, lightening the baggage. The books were the first to go. He had owned Hindi, Urdu and Bengali books, and they'd left vacant spaces on the shelves. Then there was the twelve-volume edition of Marcel Proust's *Remembrance of Things Past* published by Chatto and Windus in 1941. Only the first part of Volume 1, *Swann's Way*, and one of Volume 9, *The Captive*, inexplicably remained. *Swann's Way* had his name inscribed on the fly-leaf in his neat, decorative handwriting, with the date and place where he had bought it: 9 May 1946, Lahore. If he was giving away the set, why did he leave those two behind? *The Veiled Wanderer Marcel Proust*, a slim book by Princess Marthe Bibesco too escaped being given away. Beds, tables, sofas, radiogram, records, clothes, shoes—everything went the way of the books. He was relieved to be rid of them all. Each object was an imposition, with an oppressive history that closed in on him, occupying space and tying him down to life when his energy was concentrated on fading away, on not being. Things were a negation of this urge because objects exist, their tactility proof of their being.

And so it was that later when I tried to find signs of him around me, I realised that there were none. He was gone without a trace. He left nothing, except the paintings. He had systematically destroyed all letters and burnt any documents that had survived an earlier purge. The bundle of clothes and the Onida television tied in a checked tablecloth that he returned to Allahabad with, after having spent half his life in Delhi, were given away after he died. He hated being photographed and the pictures we had of him were old ones. He'd sold his house in Hauz Khas long ago. There was nothing left of him. No papers to be sorted out, no mess. He'd always been a neat man. He had taken care of everything before he died, as though he were covering up his tracks in the world.

A handful of relatives and acquaintances made up the small funeral procession to Rasoolabad Ghat. There were dried flowers, rose and marigold petals fallen off the shroud, strewn scantily on the driveway leading from the veranda to the gate that had been green but was now painted black. Buffeted by the breeze, they mixed with the dust and were trodden underfoot by visitors, lying about in forlorn heaps till they were cleared the next morning. A vague smell of incense lingered briefly in the room where he'd died, an evanescence swiftly overtaken by the breath of the living.

He seemed to have vanished into thin air.

On Not Writing

'Katherine Mansfield. You will be the Katherine Mansfield of Hindi.'

My father spoke slowly, placing an emphasis on each word. He seemed to be listening to a voice in his head. '*Go on, write it down*,' he insisted, as though afraid he'd forget the ten words if they were not written immediately. His eyes were on my pen as it hesitated above the notebook. Did he really expect me to write that? It was an ordinary day and I still remember it. A crow-pheasant strutted about on the lawn, its tail feathers gleaming black. A dog barked and then there was quiet. I could hear the pressure cooker going even though the kitchen was at the far back of the house.

He said this in March 1994, a few months before he died. He had lately moved back to our Allahabad home, after having lived in Delhi for more than twenty-five years. When he arrived at the Allahabad railway station early one winter morning, all he had with him were a few clothes in an old suitcase, an Onida television tied in a checked tablecloth and a sheaf of papers that he held close against his grey zipped-up cardigan, the only one that he now possessed. I'd recently returned from Melbourne, where I'd been living for the past five years. It was while I was there that I had begun to write fiction in Hindi.

My father's hair was uncombed. Clean shaven all his life, he now had a beard born of negligence. His nails were long, yellow, and a wilderness had taken over his eyes. He had grown senile. He'd stand about in doorways, having forgotten what he had come to the room for. After my mother died, he stood by her bed and looked at the quilt bunched up on it, as if he suspected that she was underneath it. Never interested in food, he developed a sweet tooth. He ate the rasagullas that were bought for him from Hira Halwai with a focused pleasure. He wiped his hand afterwards on his white dhoti. This was a father I did not know.

When I was in my late teens and still undecided which language to write in, he had told me that the language one is born into, one's mother tongue, can be the only medium for creative expression. The irony of his statement about Katherine Mansfield, that would not have escaped him earlier, now escaped him entirely. After all, I'd started writing in Hindi largely because he'd said that fiction can only be created in one's mother tongue, and here he was setting up a New Zealand-born English writer as an ideal. But looking at the changed person he had become, I could not say this to him.

For most of his life he had been a Hindi editor and critic. Off and on, he also translated from Hindi. He had written a few stories under the pen name Akalank Mehta, and they were in Hindi too. I did not know about the stories until after he died. I read a couple of them when they were published after his death in the memorial issue of *Kahani,* the journal he had edited. I realised how disappointed he must have felt after writing them. One of the things he was fond of saying was that a failed writer becomes a critic. The weight of his literary expectations had come to rest on me. 'She will go far,' he told my mother after reading the first story I had sent to him from Melbourne. He seemed happy that I was showing an inclination towards writing.

My father's statement about the mother tongue stayed with me when I started writing, late, my fiction in Hindi. Another thing that I barely acknowledged even to myself was that I felt something like shame whenever I thought of writing in English. It seemed wrong that a granddaughter of Premchand should be doing so. Our family had a certain linguistic pride. I knew that Premchand was famous, but I had not realised the extent of his popularity. In the Hindi class at St Mary's Convent School where I studied in Allahabad, the teacher would point me out to the other children when we came to the Premchand story, and everyone would turn to look at me. This was the moment I'd been dreading from the beginning of term, and now the moment had arrived. This was only the beginning. The fact of Premchand, that I was his granddaughter followed me everywhere. Everyone had a story to tell about their personal engagement with his fiction—the shopkeeper woman who went to dusty bookracks overhung with cobwebs in a dark, neglected village library in Bihar to find his books with the help of a candle; the long-time cook in my father's Delhi house, Ramchander, who wept over Premchand's story 'Alagyojha' (Divided Hearths) that he read between cooking meals; the cyclist whom we met at a wayside tea stall in Gopiganj, where we'd stopped while driving to Benares, who recited whole passages from a favourite story. The list was long, for everyone seemed to have read Premchand. Ironically, it was this very ubiquity, the reverence and love that he inspired in people, that made him something too large for me to comprehend in the early years of my life. It led also to a paradoxical feeling that, without having read it, just by being related to him I had somehow inhaled his writing! The reading happened much later.

The connection with Premchand was only one of the things that contributed to my confusion about which language to write in. And the question was never quite settled for me. I had been born into Hindustani, the mix of Hindi and Urdu that we spoke at home. We were forbidden to speak in Hindi at the English-medium school I went to, and transgressions were punished with a fine. We were embarrassed to speak in English at home. I did not know which my first language was. It felt more natural to be speaking in Hindustani. But the books I read were in English. Hindi textbooks, the ones we came across in school, despite the rare interesting story, had seen to it that we stayed off Hindi literature for a long time. It was only later, when my father needed some help in sifting through the hundreds of stories that were sent for publication in *Kahani*, that I found myself reading Hindi literature. I could write more freely in English, being accustomed to it from school. So much so that when my early stories started appearing in Hindi, someone asked me whether I had written them in Roman. As a four-year-old, I was on the lookout for simple ways to convert Hindi words into English, for I could not speak it yet—'khilao-d' 'baithao-d' 'sulao-d' (fed, seated, made to sleep)—as if merely adding a 'd' to the Hindi word made it English! The preoccupation with language went back a long way. The first story I ever wrote was in English. It was titled 'Lucky Horace'. I was eight years old at the time, and the story was modelled on the Enid Blyton books that I had read when I was very young.

While still in my teens, I'd started translating into English stories from Hindi and, later, some from Urdu and some from English into Hindi. I now see that this was all a process of fumbling, of groping for a language that could be my own. I'd wake up one morning and start writing in English, or even wake from a dream in which I found myself writing in English, much after two of my short story collections had been published in Hindi. I was in a constant state of migration. It was only later, much later that a startling realisation came to me: it was possible to write in both Hindi and English. One language did not cancel out the other. This had not occurred to me as I flitted from one to the other language, my restlessness not finding the necessary repose in either. The situation was further complicated by the Urdu factor. The Hindi taught at school, heavily influenced by Sanskrit, was the punishing, burdened language that we never used in speech. What I wrote in, indeed could write in was Hindustani, the easy mix of Hindi and Urdu that we spoke at home.

My feeling of being a migrant was not confined to language alone. I had a sense of self that was transitive at a deeper level. Used to reading from an early age, my bookish life set me apart from the people around me, particularly school friends and those I came in contact with outside the home. I seemed to be always travelling, from my world of books and the thoughts that they set in motion within me to the provincial world of Allahabad. The books I read formed the core of my deeply intimate self, and I wanted to keep it secret. I felt that if I talked about them I'd be exposed, as if I had undressed in public.

It wasn't surprising that my particular situation should make me feel that I was always in transit. I belonged to a middle class that was still marked by colonial and feudal attitudes, I had an English medium education, I wrote fiction in Hindi that connected me to a circle of Hindi readers but which few of my English-educated friends read. I was constantly moving between languages and from Hindi-reading friends to English-reading ones or those who read nothing at all, in either language. There was the Shia Muslim background of my mother and the secular Hindu one of my father, the polished Urdu of my maternal grandmother that on occasion could switch to a coarser idiom when she spoke with a servant. 'Will I wash my ass with this?'

she, with her habitual acerbity, once asked a maid who'd brought an insufficient quantity of water for her daily ritual of vazu before she started her namaz. And then there was the Avadhi of the servants at home. At school, the German nuns had a clipped English accent, and they were strict about enunciation, down to the syllable on which the stress should fall in particular words. It was a mixed pot and I was very aware of being a linguistic, literary and social itinerant.

And even as I write this, I find myself wondering why I felt the need to write about writing at all; and now that I am doing so, why is it that I choose to do so in English, when my fiction is primarily in Hindi? Could it be that I need the perspective of linguistic distance? Or is it that some things are better expressed in one language rather than another? To an extent both are true and yet neither is. Premchand did not write fiction in English. English, however, was the language he often used to draw up the extensive notes that he made before actually writing his stories in Urdu and Hindi. Can it be that the economy of English lends itself better to the conceptualisation and framing of a piece of writing? When I was writing stories that were based on local experiences of living in places like Allahabad or Delhi, the texture of things around me seemed to get woven more easily on the loom of Hindi. Yet when writing *about* the stories, about the complex process that goes into creating fiction, English was the language that came naturally to me. I had, after all, done most of my reading in it. Suddenly it all fell into place, for how else is a literary sensibility formed except through reading, which may have little or nothing to do with one's experience. I was writing about the local, but the lens that I was looking through, so to speak, was ground by the English language. It was yet another linguistic migration.

The migration could not have been particular to me. There certainly were other writers who wrote in Hindi or Marathi or

Bangla, while they read books in English. But I had not read anyone else's account, and wondered what someone else would have made of it.

My mother Zahra Rai and her sister Moghal Mahmood both wrote stories that were published in Hindi, but had first been written in Urdu. They were as talkative as my father was silent. They'd even invented a code language, with the addition of an 'f' after every consonant, and they used it when they didn't want anyone else to make sense of what they said. They were linguistic conspirators. They'd speak very quickly and the 'f' sound occurring so frequently in their speech gave it a feathery quality, as though a breeze were rustling the leaves of a tamarind or gulmohar. The sisters talked all the time about the easy flow and refinement of Urdu and recited couplets to suit every occasion. They found fault with the Urdu used by the poet Faiz, whom they admired greatly, and excused what they thought was unidiomatic, saying that this was because he was from the Punjab. They thought the Urdu spoken in Uttar Pradesh was purer. The balance of a sentence and the way a line could get 'broken' by the use of an undesired word was something they often spoke about. It strikes me only now, when they have been dead twenty-four years, that the parsing and unravelling, the stitching and unstitching of sentences which the loquacious sisters constantly engaged in, was a first lesson in the use of language.

My father wrote his critical pieces in a Hindi I found difficult to follow. He had spent some years in Calcutta and was a fluent Bangla speaker. If he found out that someone could speak Bangla, he would converse with them only in that language, rather than in Hindi. Bhojpuri was the language that he was born into, the one he always spoke with his mother Shivrani

Devi. Whenever anyone from Lamahi turned up, he would, like a fish released from an aquarium, slide into his natural element, into the waters of a river that flowed right back to his childhood.

All this is to say that I grew up hearing several languages and dialects. It is perhaps a necessary condition of living in the Subcontinent that one's awareness of language is permeated by a multiplicity of sounds. Anything written in one language must feel the presence of others. This was also one of the things that drew me to Hindi. It seemed possible to write *by ear*, to catch the sound of the spoken. What this meant was that one could use in a story, for instance, snatches of heard conversation that were sometimes in a different dialect or language. So not only could one change the register in Hindi, but also layer the writing with resonances from other languages. Writing could more easily be adapted to the milieu one was dealing with. Speech changed across classes, but the class barrier was not easy for me to cross. English, with its middle class orientation, seemed even less up to this task. It was spoken and read in India only by the English-educated elite. So, it seemed to me that writing in English would be limited in its scope right from the beginning. The same process that limited the reach of writing in English also made the world beyond these middle class homes inaccessible *to be written about*. Catching a swear word or an exclamation as it flew across the linguistic sky, or a street vendor's cry enriched with layers of cultural memory, was hard enough in Hindi; in English it seemed impossible.

Being a woman writer already excluded me from experiences that, had I been a man, could be taken for granted. For instance, it would be difficult for me to walk around a provincial North Indian town at night, to see it while it slept. It is often the case in provincial cities that women are not visible and treated as if not there at all, especially if accompanied by a man, to whom whatever is said is addressed. But then, paradoxically, a woman is also too visible, instantly noticed and stared at. It would be hard for someone not used to local norms in Allahabad to understand how the presence of a woman at a paan shop, for example, can make other customers as well as the shopkeeper uncomfortable. Women eat paan at home, but they are not expected to be seen at paan shops where men hang about, discussing local politics and the small incidents that make up the life of a provincial town. So, a chance for the ear to tune into the colloquial, the fine gradations of street speak, the hum and buzz of the everyday is lost to a woman. Other experiences, of course, are available to be written about. But truth to tell, at the time I started writing, I did not think clearly about these things. It was only an intuitive understanding of writing and what it involved. It seemed to be just something that one did, that one fell into. I realised even as a child, though without verbalising it, that this was what I would be doing. It was just a matter of being able to begin.

That was where the difficulty lay. A whole range of cultural signifiers seemed already to be given, to be kept in mind while writing—the specificity that attached to names, to caste, class and regional backgrounds. For instance, Mr Srinivasan or Mrs Gupta or Mrs Kashyap or Mr Jhunjhunwala would have their particular backgrounds, their speech moulded to a different geography of palate and tongue, their food, their style of dressing would be of their own kind. A talking parrot in a Shia Muslim, Sunni Muslim or a Hindu Kayastha household would have its own distinct speech. It was more than a question of choosing one language above another. I'd had a secluded, rather privileged upbringing in Allahabad, where the bungalows were far apart and there were few people to interact with. There was no class of society that I could honestly say I knew well. I was on an island and seemed to be the sole inhabitant. Instinct told me that a writer lived within me, but it appeared that the writer had neither the material to write about, nor the language to write it in.

In all the years that I spent not writing, there was ample time to think—about words, their interactions with other words. And while I was fumbling to find my voice, I realised that the Sanskrit-derived Hindi word *shabd* had a double meaning. It meant 'word', but it also meant 'sound'. This seemed serendipitous to me. The first time I learnt about its two meanings, the word drew for me a connection between written language and language that was only sound. The creaking of the wheels of a bullock-cart in Chhattisgarh, on which I got the chance to take a ride; the hollow sound of a hand-pump being worked; the whistle of a train engine—this was a language of sound that did not lead to further meaning. It was simply itself. Somehow this had implications for a writer.

It occurred to me that the double meaning of the word *shabd* had created for me a bridge between the heard and the written, that the craft of writing is auditory as much as it is visual. That a sentence or a paragraph, when it is written, must be *heard* as well as seen.

On the morning when he made the extraordinary Katherine Mansfield statement, my father and I were sitting on the front veranda. The ground outside was sodden, the air saturated with moisture. It had been raining, though it was not the rainy season. The Mary Palmer growing right outside the veranda had pink and white blossoms. The rain had shaken loose the flowers and they had collected in the shallow water-race that ran round the house, looking profuse yet forlorn. Termites had silently been eating the books on the glass-fronted bookshelf in the drawing room that opened out onto the veranda. The spines were intact, but the pages had been hollowed out in the shape of ridges and terraces. I had spread them out on the veranda floor, pages open, to air them. There were a lot of books. Most of them were my father's, left behind in the Allahabad house when he'd moved to Delhi; he'd given away the ones he had there.

There was Oscar Wilde's *De Profundis*; a battered illustrated *Arabian Nights*; the Everyman's Library edition, published in 1929, of Abbé Prévost's *Manon Lescaut*; Prosper Mérimée's *Carmen*; *The Collected Stories of Katherine Mansfield*; and two of the twelve volumes of *Remembrance of Things Past*, published by Chatto and Windus in 1941. The bright orange dust jacket of *Marcel Proust: A Selection from his Miscellaneous Writings Chosen and Translated by Gerard Hopkins* had been eaten away by termites. What was left of the book crumbled first into paper flakes and then to dust when I tried to leaf through it. *Gitobitan*, the fat volume containing the songs of Rabindranath Tagore, was intact, as was the English translation of Premchand's *Godan* by Gordon Roadarmel, published as *The Gift of a Cow* by Allen and Unwin in 1968. My father stood in the midst of these books, like a battle-weary king looking at his ruined palace.

Some of the books that lay open on the veranda—*Treasure Island* and *Alice in Wonderland* among them—were the ones I had grown up reading. I was a little like a termite myself. I ate the words, the physical form of the words, though unlike a termite without quite ingesting them. The books in the drawing room were housed in two shelves with sliding glass fronts and in two teakwood cupboards. The cupboards were built into the wall on either side of a blocked-up fireplace, whose mantelpiece was made of pale pink terrazzo. The doors of the cupboards tended to get stuck. When pulled open, there rose from inside a smell of fresh varnish, even though it was years since the painters had finished their job.

As a child, I'd developed a fascination for the written word, regardless of where I saw it. I read train timetables, dictionaries, cinema hoardings and shop signs. Allahabad roads had signposts with their names on them—Thornhill, Clive, Elgin, Hastings, Edmonstone—and each name seemed to have a distinctive colour and shape. I read the graffiti on the exposed brick walls that we passed on the slow train journeys that we undertook between Allahabad and Benares or between Allahabad and Delhi. My eye caught the names of the stations, written in black on a sunflower-yellow background in three languages, Hindi, English and Urdu: Handia, Jangiganj, Kachchwa Road, Madhosingh, Raja Talab, Manduadih. The names stayed in my visual memory long after the train had reached its destination.

It was while travelling through the bookish landscape, which I first became acquainted with in childhood, that I made an extraordinary discovery. *All the books were about me.* They were set in locations thousands of miles away—St Petersburg, London, New York, Paris or Rouen—and yet they spoke of things that I could have said. This was something that stirred me into restless excitement. Could I create a fictional world of my own? Many years later, while reading Proust's essay 'Days of Reading', I came to understand how inextricably reading and writing were linked:

> The lazy mind can get nothing from *pure* solitude, because it is incapable, unaided, of getting its creative activity to work .... What, then, is needed is some sort of intervention, which, though it may come from elsewhere, does stir the requisite consciousness in ourselves, an impulse having its origin outside ourselves, but received into the very centre of our personal loneliness. This is the true definition of reading, and it fits no other activity.

The books that I read also led me to put on a certain weary pose, a kind of melancholic despairing stance that I associated with Kafka which, given my circumstances, was quite absurd. I was always writing a diary. I waited to get to it, and when I did, what emerged from my pen was a stream of regurgitation from the stuff that I had been reading. In a diary entry from age nineteen, I found:

> Pessimism, fear, humiliation—so many reasons to make one feel heavy-hearted. The day is spent in mundane doings. The eyes are useless, being employed only in staring at nothingness.

In my bookish life, the characters and landscapes in the novels that I read were more real than the people I actually met. It was an imaginative world inhabited by fictive characters and their milieu, and it became a barrier between me and the world I lived in. No one else seemed to care about books or writing, and I was not interested in the things that mattered to them. The questions that plagued me—'Will I ever be able to write? And if not, what then?'—would to them have sounded laughable. My agonising about writing went on for a long time. In a diary entry from 6 June 1976, I found:

> One needs to be alone to write. If you want to write, there is just one way—write. Acquire the habit of writing. Only when this initial stage is crossed, does the eye become discerning and the brain perceptive.

A month later I wrote:

> It is impossible that I can go on existing like this, dreaming, struggling to stop dreaming and to actually give expression to the many voices in my brain. I cannot go on like this much longer. Writing has become a question of life and death.

But as things stood, I spent years searching for the writer in me who was nowhere to be seen. It was like having a star-crossed lover. The writer and I could never meet. I would look at the shape of my hands to see if they looked like a writer's. I stared into my eyes in the mirror, wondering if they would reveal to me the writer that I was convinced I was, though there was little evidence to support this idea. When my father asked me to write down the words about Katherine Mansfield, one of my Hindi short story collections had already been published. But that was where my writing aspirations seemed to have ended. I hadn't written a thing in months. And here was my father, asking me to do something more than just writing those words down. Something too large for me to grasp, something that I kept trying to escape from and that kept escaping from me, slipping through my fingers like glittering particles of mica. I wanted to hold on to it even as I wanted to flee from it. My flight from the act of writing fiction went on for years. I could not face it. I thought that writing was all about not writing.

It was after my father died that I wrote in my story 'Biyabaan Mein' (In the Wilderness) about the struggle that writing fiction was for me:

> I try to write. I want to focus my attention on writing. But my mind is empty like the sky that stretches in front of me. Sometimes groups of broken sentences, indistinct faces, the rags of days long past move across my mind in a procession. I am unable to grasp the forms and mould them into something that is whole. The images fly away into the sky like birds.

It was a long time before I realised that the process of writing begins much before one has put anything down; that one has, so to speak, always been writing. It was while chasing butterflies in the garden as a child, or watching a tortoise-shell cat slink away into a dark alley, that the writing was taking place. Like an invisible letter written with lime juice, that only shows up when a hot iron is put to it, the impressions that have been written on to the memory all the while that life is being lived are revealed in the catalysing moment when pen meets paper. The city buried underground and long forgotten about is chanced upon, and not without a shock of surprise. And so it was, that years after the house of my childhood had slipped into oblivion, I found myself writing:

> Suddenly there was an army of mice in the house. The signs of their presence could be found in all the rooms, and especially in the storeroom. The scraps of nibbled paper, the pieces of roti, the mouse droppings inside the cupboards, under the chairs and behind the black iron trunk, were evidence of their being around.

When I wrote those words, the colour of the light from that buried time, the clinking sound of the bunch of keys that my mother carried tucked into her sari, the whole breathing quality of the house as it was then, came back to me as though the past could never quite be past.

Recently, I found the ten words that had been uttered by my father twenty-three years ago, written in the orange notebook I had been using at the time, the long letters sloping to the left, the handwriting uncertain.

Future Perfect

The shifting montage of buff, black, tan and greys in the opaque interior of my brother's closet appeared to be saying something. They were shoes. He had an obsession with shoes and he'd collected quite a few. There were cap toe oxfords and plain ones, brogues, lace-ups and slip-ons, loafers, moccasins, wingtips—of suede, which did not need to be polished, and leather, which did. It wasn't as if he needed more shoes, but once in a few months, he'd visit alternately the two Chinese shoemakers, both in Civil Lines, one of them called Wanson and the other Fookson, to have his feet measured for handmade shoes of calf leather. He never wore the oxfords without polishing them, and if Shankar, the helper whose job it was to polish the shoes, hadn't done them already, he'd settle down half an hour before he had to go out with the shoebox that held the paraphernalia needed for the task, including the small flat jars of Cherry Blossom Boot Polish and hog hair brushes. When he wasn't wearing them, the moccasins with their foot-shaped emptiness cried out his absence. My brother did not display a similar fondness for any other object or person and never spoke about his desires.

The closest he'd come to an attachment of this sort was to his Raleigh bicycle that he rode to school and on which he practised slow cycling at home, whistling softly as he tried to keep his balance. He cleaned the bike every day, rubbing it with a wet rag till it glistened, all shiny handlebars and mudguards, and it stood outside the back veranda looking like a strange metallic animal catching the light of the sun. When we were children, my mother asked him if there was a particular item of food that he felt like eating or if there was, for instance, any *razai* that he preferred from the ones that had been embroidered and sent at the onset of winter from Banaras by our grandmother. But he never had a clear choice, so she kept aside for him the one she thought was the best, just in case. He spoke little and seemed to be as calm as the sea at low tide, but this was not so with his shoes; you could almost hear the dry whispering sound of the restlessness that they exuded. Stacked up in the cupboard and fallen out of it when there was no more room, they smelt of other places, as if they were eager to get going. If on the one hand, the shoes proclaimed the fixity of the ground on which they stood, on the other they spoke of movement and the distances that they might walk to.

For my brother distances lay in the future; after all they were 'there' rather than 'here', located in an unspecified time that was 'when' or 'then', not now. Everything that mattered to him was in the future. The present was of little concern, being only the necessary passage to the time when his abstract longings would be fulfilled and his frequently renewed schemes for making money, grand till he lost interest in them, would come to fruition. The unnamed despair that he was prey to would then be known for what it was, and dealt with. But this, the future time when he hoped his crises would be resolved seemed already to be upon him, and it presented no appeasement of his vague frustrations. Time was going by and he had achieved nothing. 'In eleven years, I'll be forty!' he cried out one morning when he was particularly beset by anguish, the absurdity of the statement bringing a smile to my mother's face. He was interested in the idea of money rather than the money itself, which for him held little value; he had hardly any use for it and even less respect. That is, he had no personal use for money, but it still flowed through his fingers like sand, for it didn't take long for a circle of 'needy' friends and hangers-on to gather around him. He had a tender heart—when he was three or four years old, he'd cry inconsolably if someone, in order to tease him, pointed out to him that his grandmother's shoe was torn, or that the random man passing by on the street had no money for his next meal.

He had missed the birth anniversary of Rabindranath Tagore by a day, having been born on 8 May 1949, eighty-eight years after Tagore. The month was the same and the date close enough to the poet's for my father to feel a certain pride and joy at this serendipity. He must have felt, though he never actually said it, that his son had been born under the same star as the great man and was possibly also destined to be great. My father was a Tagore aficionado and had been present at his funeral. In later years, he realised that nothing was going to come of his expectations from his eldest offspring even though in the combination of looks, health, and brains, nature seemed to have favoured him. You give him ten rupees or ten million he'll run through both in a day, was what he said about his son when it had become clear that he would indefinitely have to finance him and as it soon turned out, his wife as well.

He had fallen in love with a Pakistani girl, a medical student, who was visiting relatives in India, and it took him no time to promise that he would marry her when she visited next from Karachi after completing her studies. Absence is said to make the heart grow fonder, but he only developed cold feet and soon tried to back out of the commitment so rashly given. However, he was persuaded by his father, for whom a promise was a promise, to keep his word, and a few years later a nikah took place in Delhi. The ceremony was attended by no one from the family because our grandmother had died in Allahabad two days before the wedding. My father in a display of emotion rare for him cried out that with his mother no longer in it, his world had grown dark, and he left immediately for Allahabad to see to the death rituals.

It looked as if it would be quite a while before my brother started earning his own money. To earn, he first had to invest. The various money-making schemes that he came up with—catfish cultivation, the procurement of government orders for the books he intended to publish under various imprints, the setting up of a small company, Graab Electromechs, to make thermal fuses with technical help from two engineer friends who were his business partners—all needed capital. And how else could he find the money except by asking his father? But the 'dream' projects continued long after my father died—the buying of a lathe machine to manufacture various items of plastic in a 'factory' with a tarpaulin roof that was set up in the grounds of our Allahabad house, a commercial scheme for rainwater harvesting, the making of a basic computer for use in village schools—he was full of ideas, his nimble mind moved from one scheme to the next when the previous one showed signs of failing. His fresh involvements kept unfurling like new leaves on a deciduous tree that grows the leaves only to shed them in autumn. The failure to stick to any one thing for long—a lack of 'stickability' was his own phrase for it—was the fatal flaw in his make-up and it wrote his destiny.

In line with the pattern set early by his having missed by a day Tagore's birthday, he kept missing success by a whisker, and since he had borrowed large sums of money for the scheme current at the time—which in the event turned out to be harebrained—it landed him in debt to all sorts of dubious characters. But it wasn't as if he made no money at all. In the early years, the first order for thermal fuses finalised by Graab Electromechs brought in a substantial amount because the margin of profit in making the fuses was high. But the money soon trickled away—where did it go? Well, some of it went into the next project, which was the creation of the TV series *Nirmala* based on the novel by Premchand whose copyright was still held by our family. My brother had no expertise in this area, but he had an infallible sense of language, which made the writing of the screenplay easier, and his involvement in the project meant that the copyright hurdle could be crossed easily. He was also willing to put into the project his share of the profits from Graab, so his colleagues on the show found that associating with him had several advantages. To add to that, he was an agreeable person to have around.

The modest success of *Nirmala* brought about no improvement in his personal fortunes, however; he continued to wear like a second skin the one Pathan suit that he owned, which consisted of a long black kurta and a black salwar. There'd been the years when he wore trousers, white shirts and a buff green suede jacket that he lived in. Then, he seemed to have endless amounts of time to spend at his toilette, locked away in the bathroom at the back of the Drummond Road house. He'd emerge from it in a cloud of Tabac aftershave, his cheeks smooth and hair carefully combed. But those days were over. He was in Delhi now and had become careless about his appearance. Even so, he was tall, thin, and rather handsome. The black outfit that he wore heightened the romantic, somewhat Hamlet-like melancholy that hung about him which, combined with his shy smile and self-deprecating manner, made him irresistibly attractive to women. He'd already been involved with several, and by now he had a failed marriage behind him too. There was no reason why he wouldn't notice the dusky female lead in *Nirmala,* and his affair with her seemed to be the only thing that came out of the whole enterprise.

Sometimes, with a rueful smile, he'd spread out both his hands and show us the fine whorls of lines shaped like shells that made up his fingerprints—'shankhs'—that swirled and eddied without forming a circle with a distinct centre, for a circle was a 'chakra', and if he had ten chakras on his fingers, it would mean that he was destined one day to be a 'chakravarti' or king. Even four or five chakras denoted money, but what he had instead were 'shankhs' in all ten fingers, the shells signifying that he would become a sadhu, and in those days, sadhus were still associated with spiritualism and deemed to have no worldly possessions. The 'godmen' with their questionable wealth that captured the imagination of many in the middle class were still in the future. It could all have been put down to fate, except for the fact that his father's fingers too had ten 'shankhs'. But this had not prevented him from creating a small business empire, even if he did lose all his money at the end of his life. It wasn't as if my brother believed in all this mumbo jumbo. It was a sort of game, an impatience to see into the future, and if the time that he anticipated turned out not to be acceptable to him, he could have the excuse that it was all the fault of the 'shankhs' that clearly had been at work.

His parents and especially the father certainly had a hand in the shaping of the son's story. Watched over by them with solicitous attention from the days of his infancy, each little fact noted about him became a cause for worry or for jubilation. When the two-year-old said that the trees around him were *'lal lal'*—all red—they worried that he was going to turn out colour blind. At the age of four he seemed to be gaining unwelcome weight and was taken to the homeopathic physician whom my father believed in with something akin to religious fervour. The homeopath said that the boy was definitely obese and that his constitution would have to be changed. The medication he prescribed to bring this about proved surprisingly effective, and confirming my father's faith in the homeopath, my brother never put on an extra ounce of flesh all his life.

He'd been slow at starting to walk, but he learnt other forms of locomotion with an unusual quickness—by the time he was eleven, he could drive my father's Studebaker Commander, the long silver-finned car that stood in the portico and was something of a novelty in the Allahabad of the sixties with its narrow and potholed roads. At first, he drove it up to the gate and backed it slowly into the porch, then he started going out of the gate. He'd get up at dawn before the rest of the family woke up and, as he told us later, head for the deserted cantonment area. He'd learnt to drive simply by observing our father; it's still a mystery how he got hold of the car keys. Soon he could drive, barely visible from outside above the steering wheel, the Studebaker Pickup in which our father drove us to the hills, to Ranikhet or Mussoorie in the summer. Cars became an abiding passion with him and he was a stylish driver. But he never learnt to drive slowly like our father; behind the wheel a certain recklessness took hold of him and the speed at which he drove caused my father sitting beside him to clench his muscles and, with an intake of breath, say, 'Can't you go slow? No idiot could come under the wheels of *my* car even if he was trying to commit suicide!' During his university days, the Studebaker was the only car of its kind that could be seen on the campus, and a small admiring crowd of fellow students would gather as he parked it in front of the Senate Hall or, aware of the watching eyes, deliberately cut a figure of eight on his way out. In later years, we'd hold our breath as he drove on tricky narrow mountain roads that had no culverts to separate them from the sheer drop down the hillside.

He'd been brought up not to know want of any kind. In his late teens and early twenties, he had access, not similarly offered to his siblings who may have been too young then, to my father's accounts in the shops considered expensive in Allahabad in those days. This meant that he could buy anything just by signing for it; the physical handling of money was considered indelicate, even vulgar. It was not the age of credit cards, but he had a credit card of sorts all the same. A desire for something—books, records, clothes, shoes, aftershaves, cigarettes, anything really—could be satisfied even before it had been recognised as a desire, and it resulted in his growing up confused about what it was that he really wanted. Though he soon came to know of one particular thing that he did want. Hesitantly at first, he had started signing for whisky at Khunnoolal's in Civil Lines unbeknownst to his father who was now regularly travelling between Allahabad and Delhi, living first on rent in Defence Colony and then in South Extension till he bought his own house in Hauz Khas into which he moved in the late sixties. My brother followed him a few years later. He had completed his Masters and could now be expected to help my father in the publishing business.

A new cubicle was designed for him at the Saraswati Press office in Daryaganj, set up with a large desk equipped with files, paperweights, rubber stamps, inkstands, penholders, paperknives, pencils and erasers et al., the entire place lined with bookshelves—for there was certainly no dearth of books—so that he could work undisturbed. But that was the trouble. He did not know the nature of the work he was supposed to do. My father, having started out on his own career not hesitating to do even menial jobs like tying book bundles and sticking stamps on correspondence, had considerably expanded the business which now had offices in several towns. But he was used to a one-man show and didn't quite know what jobs he could assign to his son who was certainly not going to sit around the whole day in his cubicle licking stamps, which, especially now that there were others to do this, really amounted to twiddling his thumbs. But what with the tendency for money to vanish from his hands, could he really be trusted in a position where he controlled the finances? Quite rapidly an impasse was reached. The father's grouse was that the son didn't do anything useful, and the son's that he wasn't allowed to do anything meaningful, by which he meant basically anything that required decisions about how and where money was to be spent. So, while conditions were created for him to be able to work at Saraswati Press, a separate situation too seemed simultaneously to be in place in which he couldn't.

A compromise of sorts was made and a new imprint for academic books in English was initiated in my brother's name—Atul Prakashan—and the only book to emerge from there in 1975 was *Israeli Soviet Cold War* by Surendra Bhutani, modestly priced at Rs 56. This was also the time when *Acta Anthropogenetica*, an international journal of research in human genetics, originally published by the University of California, was appearing from Saraswati Press. My brother collaborated on this project with our cousin, my father's sister's son Prabodh Kumar Shrivastava. Prabodh, who taught genetics at the Punjabi University of Patiala, sporadically wrote for the journal, and it was because of him that *Acta Anthropogenetica* was published from Saraswati Press. He was a man of quiet intelligence, also a Hindi litterateur who had a strong affinity with my father and got along well with my brother. But even here, my brother was not certain what his role in the project was, and soon he got distanced from it.

He would reach the Daryaganj office with alacrity, beating the rush hour traffic, but then sit in his cubicle all day doing nothing and bored out of his mind, wondering what his next project should be. It was in these long days of idleness that he discovered the usefulness of alcohol as a panacea for his angst. It seemed to do him good—the dissatisfactions of his life faded. It was as if he stood on top of a hill and had only to reach up his arms to grab the sky. Things rapidly came to such a pass that he felt a sense of well-being only when he was drunk. He drank when he was alone, and he drank surreptitiously when he was with people, the need for secrecy making it necessary for him to hide in a convenient corner to polish off neat, in a few hurried swigs, the quarter or half bought from the government shop, and he'd emerge afterwards with eyes shining unnaturally, talking more than usual.

His father who now found the long drive to Daryaganj tiring only put in rare appearances at the office, and this cleared the ground for my brother's drinking buddies to meet there regularly for binge sessions. The same friends dropped by at home as well, and soon my father's long-time cook Ramchander, a dignified and somewhat rotund gentleman whom we called Shakespeare because of his uncanny resemblance to the poet, started panting up the stairs to my brother's room, carrying trays with glasses and ice buckets. The friends composed quite a menagerie. There was Battle Tank, a Punjabi businessman who'd earned the nickname because of his vast size and because he was an alcohol tank of sorts. He wore trousers that had been specially tailored with enormous pockets that could accommodate, on either side, a bottle of Johnnie Walker Magnum, and he'd arrive early in the evening, making soft sloshing and clinking sounds that caused the eyes of the initiated to light up. When he was drunk enough and inspired enough, he'd get up on to the table that was apparently sturdier than it looked and dance. One of the other regulars was a refined Kashmiri with a literary bent of mind and fountains of hair sprouting from his ears. He joined the gang to get away from his three rather large dragon sisters who ruled him with an iron hand. The misfortunes of his life melted into poetry, and as the evening progressed, he'd recite quite unstoppably in his booming voice the Urdu couplets that he had composed. My father, who would be in the adjacent room, was too discreet to intrude on the jollity despite all the commotion. Then there was Mouse, who was small and could hide in the wardrobe when his strident wife came looking for him. My brother had a natural propensity to hide anyway, and so he too tried to conceal himself behind the table, which turned out not to be high enough for the purpose. He was spotted at once and made to give uncomfortable explanations.

It was around this time that he discovered western classical music. The lane behind our Hauz Khas house that led to the market went past the house of K.K. Nair, the music and dance critic who wrote under the pseudonym of Krishna Chaitanya. Always dressed in a printed khadi dressing gown, wearing thick black-framed glasses and with a cigar hanging from his blue lips, Nair could often be seen leaning on his gate watching the passersby. On one of these days, my brother, who was walking past, stopped when he heard the strains of the most captivating music he had heard emanating from K.K. Nair's house. His eyes met the critic's. No conversation took place between them then or thereafter, except for the one cryptic word that K.K. Nair enunciated with his heavy Malayali accent: '*Ai-den*'. This silent encounter between the seasoned music lover and the newly initiated one was often repeated, and it was only after several meetings of this kind and some familiarity with the famous western classical music composers that my brother figured out the one mysterious word that had passed between them. Haydn.

In the meantime, his wife, tired of playing nurse to a man who she said did nothing but lie in bed reeking of alcohol and staring at the ceiling, packed up and left for Karachi, taking along with her their two-year-old daughter. This plunged him into further despair but did nothing to help him kick the habit that had landed him in this mess. Rather it exacerbated his dependence on alcohol. Once, looking for something, I opened the cupboard in his room and an avalanche of empty bottles clattered to the floor. There were times when my mother who was visiting from Allahabad would ask me to go check up on him, to see if he was okay. On one such occasion I found him lying in bed, but he sat up when he saw me and quite out of the blue startled me by saying in a low, urgent tone, '*These days I'm selling my blood to stay alive.*' I did not know how to react to this, whether to believe what he said or not, for telling lies came naturally to him and he did it with a straight face. I did not ask him where he did the transaction and how much he got for it—after all, I didn't want to embarrass him by having to explain something he'd feel silly about when he was sober. Nor did I tell anyone about what he'd said to me.

My father, at this point, perhaps out of desperation, began to believe that things might go better for his son if he was not constantly under the father's watchful eye. So he set him up in a rented barsati that belonged to Kartarsingh Duggal at the far end of Hauz Khas with Trivenipal, one of the clerks from Saraswati Press, for company. This brought temporary relief from anxiety to my father, but whatever his plan may have been, it didn't work. Trivenipal became my brother's Man Friday cum drinking buddy, and the barsati became a regular hangout for his companions. Besides, it was a drain on the family resources, and since it wasn't serving its purpose anyway, the place was soon relinquished, my brother was back at home, and things settled once again into the familiar pattern.

But then, in November 1987, the father wrote a letter to his son, one written 'most unwillingly and with a very sad heart'. Its deliberate implacability was heartbreaking for the effort it must have taken him to direct this harshness at a son so doted upon. Beneath the carefully formed floral handwriting lay the white expanse of the unwritten—the avidly nurtured love, the pride in his son's capabilities, the expectations that had come to nought—but more than all of these, there was the close identification with him. If the son failed at anything, it was the father who had failed. And he was 'not given to failure, nor did he accept it with grace'. This view of the father and the son being somehow conjoined also pointed to his egotism, for he could not think of his son as a separate entity. Whatever the son did was a result of the father's sins, which he 'still hoped to expiate'. It was, he said, his son's weakness for alcohol that had destroyed him 'body and soul', and even if he attained worldly success, it would mean nothing. My father too was used to his evening drink, which he imbibed in homeopathic doses, but he drew a distinction between the two; he called himself a drunkard, whereas the son was an alcoholic. The advice he offered to his son right at the end of the letter was to 'take it that your father is dead and you have to live your life on your own.' In order to do this, he would have to go back to Allahabad to be in the care of his mother who had preferred not to move to Delhi. In any case, in ways never quite acknowledged, he blamed her aristocratic background and the tendencies inherited from there for the condition that the son now found himself in. It must have taken courage to write the letter, and in it, he exhorted the son also to have the courage to regenerate his lost self-confidence and sanity. By no means did he intend this to be a permanent move—three months was the time he stipulated in which the son would have 'returned to sanity'.

Subsequently, my brother did return to sanity but not to Delhi. He hit upon several other projects to grab by the tail his life of under achievement as it rushed by. In these years, he came close to his mother, and they'd sit for hours in the front veranda of our Drummond Road house in Allahabad, drinking endless cups of tea, the spoon tinkling in the bone china cup as they stirred the brew, talking about all manner of things. His early fondness for shoes had now settled onto a small shoe-shaped ashtray made of brass in which he kept tipping the ash from his cigarette, while he sat there chatting with his mother. He married again and a new daughter was born, and this time both wife and daughter stayed. He rarely emerged from his rooms now, and when there was a 'sighting', people joked that he had been given an 'out pass', for they believed that it was his wife who kept him caged. If that was the case, he came to love his cage in time, and looked uncomfortable when he stepped out of it. It was not simply that he had missed success, he had also missed himself. Muddling along through life, he had failed to recognise his deepest impulses.

It was during the 'caged' years that on New Year's Day 2000 he asked me, for he did not have internet, to send an email to his first daughter who was now almost twenty-one years old. It was a difficult filial love that had haunted him ever since she went away with her mother at the age of two. He stood by as I typed the 'secret' letter that he did not want his wife to see:

> Along with apologies for not being able to write to you earlier, I would like to convey to you my fondest wishes for a very happy new year. I hope that you enjoyed yourself to the hilt. As for myself, I have ushered in the new year keeping my fingers

> crossed. The last few years have been so bad for me that I can only think of new years with some trepidation. Your letter was brief, mine was briefer. I would like to get a much longer letter from you, which I think is not unreasonable as life for me gets less and less exciting as I grow older, whereas for you, at the lovely stage of life you are at, it is full of excitement. That's how we come to the conclusion that it's you who should write longer letters....'

He'd taken to walking at a set time in the early evening on the cemented drive that ran round the house, pausing briefly to touch what looked to anyone watching like private totems—the trunk of a silver oak or the jasmine trellis at one end of the drive. It was in 2013 during these walks that he began to show the first signs of a baffling disease that predisposed him to frequent falls. His eyes grew fixed, his speech encumbered, and he steadily lost weight. It was mistaken for Parkinson's but was eventually diagnosed as PSP or progressive supra nuclear palsy, an obscure and incurable ailment that affected the central nervous system. He spent his last years in one of the smallest of the sixteen rooms in the bungalow. The few times he left his bed was when he was helped into a straight-backed chair for his meals that became smaller with the passage of the days. It was on one of these occasions when he was sitting up in the chair that he, who had gone through life not knowing what it was that he wanted and certainly did not voice it if he did, finally expressed a desire.

He'd like to go to the hills, he said haltingly, with a ghost of his disarming smile—to Ranikhet, to see the old places again ...

He died a few weeks later. Among the effects that he left behind, were three large trunks in the gallery that ran the breadth of the house. One of them was big enough to accommodate three adults. Apart from mothballed clothes, vases and candle stands, there was the tea caddy that had held flowery orange pekoe, along with the teapot and the tea cosy which had become frayed with use. The container for sugar with its high top remained, but the cups and the milk jug from the set had not survived. Most of the trunk was filled with books—Kipling's *Kim* and Alan Paton's *Cry the Beloved Country* fell out when I lifted the lid of the trunk. My brother had been addicted to the written word; he read encyclopaedias, dictionaries, even train timetables. He pored over maps in outdated atlases—the *Caxton Atlas of the Earth* was buried at the bottom of the trunk. He'd read out from it the resonant names of places we hadn't heard of—Bahr el Ghazal, Asmara, Izmir, Tananarive. And yet, many of the books in the trunk looked unread.

Something strange had happened. A very large painting by my father, damaged and with most of the paint peeled off, had fallen from up high in the gallery where it had been hung. Somehow it had landed straight in the narrow gap behind the trunks, as if it had always been stacked there on purpose; except that it hadn't been stacked the way paintings usually are, facing the wall. It wasn't facing the wall. From the height at which it had been hung, it had fallen straight with its face forward. Beneath the parts where the oil paint had worn off, a complex pattern of lines and smudges had emerged on the bald discoloured canvas, like a secret code that had remained hidden all these years but was now there for everyone to see. In the gap between the trunks and the wall, I also found the dumb bells and the heavy wooden clubs that had belonged to my brother—he had given them up years ago. He'd been, when young, a fitness freak. No one seemed to have cleaned behind the trunks in a long time. The dumb bells and the clubs were covered with dust and cobwebs.

The rusty trunks stood in the gallery for years. No one quite knew what to do with them, and since they seemed to serve no purpose, they were finally given away, along with their contents, to the rag-and-bone man the next time he came round. He stacked the books up high on his tarazu, using five stones as weight measures. It took him an hour to get through the lot. He paid seven rupees per kilo, counting out the notes carefully from a grubby little bundle that he drew from the pocket of his pants.

Old Blood

'I already told you she's dead,' said the doctor on duty when he looked inside the Fiat.

He seemed confused and he was not to be blamed for it. A few hours earlier, we had brought my aunt to the same emergency wing of the Kabir Chaura Hospital in Banaras in the same car. The same doctor had been on duty then too, and he had declared her dead. He did not realise now that it was a different woman. To a stranger they must have looked similar—around the same age, build and complexion. It was my mother this time. She'd been told that her sister, our aunt Moghal Mahmood, had had a heart attack just as she was getting ready to sleep, that she was now dead and was in the room where my grandmother had lived when she was alive. It was their Nawab-ki-Deorhi home in Banaras where they'd been born and had grown up together and which we were now visiting from Allahabad. It proved too much for my mother. Not one to lag behind her sister, she had a stroke later that night as she lay alone in the big room adjoining the courtyard, while the rest of us sat surrounding my recently deceased aunt as though waiting for her to wake up. It was 2 a.m. when I found my mother, who seemed to have slipped into a coma.

As we drove to the hospital, I had the feeling, familiar to me from dreams, that all of this—getting an inert body into the back seat of the car that was too small, the panic, the hurry in which we didn't think to grab a sweater on the way out on that cold night—had happened before. But this was no dream. It was the same road that we had been on a few hours earlier. The narrow road, with small shops on one side of it and a wide shallow drain on the other, which was crowded with traffic during the day was deserted. It was not a full moon night. The car swerved to the left to avoid a heap of garbage—broken kulhars and leaf-plates, twigs, putrid muck from the drain—piled up by the side of the road making it narrower. There were dogs sitting on long parapets outside the shops that had their shutters pulled down. You could see the dogs' ribs, their thin tails. A leafless tree on the roof of one of the shops cast a shadow on the road. There was no sound. The still scene looked like a Dali painting. Images of a clock melting and a lobster perched on a telephone floated into my head. Something was ticking with a ragged rhythm. It was my heart. We were in a terrible rush. There was no time to make sense of anything.

They laid my mother on a stretcher on the floor, outside the entrance to the emergency wing. The doctor, who by now had realised his mistake, pounded her chest with his fist; an assistant joined him. Maybe her heart would come around. It didn't. Her blouse had been torn in the effort to revive her and her breasts, exposed in their sudden whiteness, seemed to have lost in death a claim to the dignity of clothing. Until now we had never seen even her upper arms bare, for she didn't like wearing sleeveless blouses. My sister and I stood there, stunned; it was as if we did not know how to move, until one of us pulled her shawl over her. It was the hesitation of that moment—of letting her lie there uncovered, even if for a few minutes—that kept returning to fill me with a posthumous disquiet.

It was the last day of December, with pale sunshine that had a shard of ice lodged in its heart. There was early morning dew on the chrysanthemums. The deep pink winter leaves of the wild almond near the high corrugated tin gate became pock-marked and fell off one by one. There was frost at night. My mother and my aunt had missed 1994 by a day. Old-fashioned, natural deaths at home—no road accident, bomb blast, tsunami, earthquake or pandemic, deaths not unpredictable, for heart disease and diabetes follow an expected pattern. Two sisters dying within a few hours of each other—it could seem strange, this consecutiveness of departure. But they'd been inseparable, close in age and affection, so there was nothing in the least surprising about the manner of their dying. In fact, it seemed rather appropriate. Signs and portents were noted afterwards and commented upon, the superstitions that hover not too far from scenes of death—a pair of slippers lying one on top of the other, dead ancestors calling out in the previous night's dream, the two 'holy' shrouds that my aunt had brought back by mistake instead of one when she went on a Hajj to Mecca—invisible patterns all, that some later claimed were made by spirits that move about unseen, crisscrossing the air. But no one thought of them then, it was not the time to think of indiscernible patterns or of spirits; the dead were still in the house. The toothbrushes that they had used the previous night before going to bed were still wet, standing in the jar in front of the mirror in the bathroom.

It was an inconvenient day to die on: New Year's Eve. The mourners that streamed in must have had other things—celebrations, new beginnings and not endings—on their minds. They went inside and emerged wiping their eyes, extolling the virtues of the two sisters. The rituals took up most of New Year's Day. People sat huddled together on hurriedly set out chairs, their whispers rustling like paper. Three fat women sat in a row with their heads covered in shawls, saying nothing at all.

They turned their heads in the direction of anyone who spoke, following with their eyes the movement of speech. I noticed, suddenly very aware of the trivial, that there was a front tooth missing in the betel-stained mouth of the woman sitting to my left.

A hearse arrived from the hospital, and my brothers, along with a few other relatives, from Allahabad. It was three o'clock in the afternoon when they left for Dargah-e-Faatmaan, the shrine with its attached graveyard where most of the family's ancestors were buried. Wind blew through the empty house. They'd gone, but somehow, they were still around; it was just that they could not be reached. In a curious way, I felt a sense of relief. The unthinkable moment dreaded since childhood had come and gone. It could not come again. They could not die a second time. This was it. I visited the graves a couple of years later with flowers from the gardens that they had tended—stalks of gladioli from the Drummond Road flowerbeds and frangipani, roses and jasmine from the vine that covered the front of the Nawab-ki-Deorhi house. My mother's grave had sunk into the ground after two rainy seasons, and the marble tombstone with her name and dates of birth and death was only partially visible, but the graves of my aunt and my grandmother were intact. My cousin mumbled a fatiha, a prayer for the dead, while I stood there silently beside her, with no idea how to pray or to shed a tear.

I was no stranger to death. The June deaths, as we later referred to them, had plagued my childhood. For four years in a row, there had been a death in the family in June. We dreaded the arrival of this month, and after the third year, a death in June seemed inevitable. But all these deaths—of a brother, a cousin, a great-grandmother, an uncle, and many years later, in 1985, of another cousin who died on a train in the middle of nowhere, taking the tally of June deaths to five—took place somewhere else, not where I was, in our Allahabad house. There was the fact of death but not the physical validation of it. I had never seen a dead person. As children we had been shielded from the sight of death. My mother, and, in fact, all the relatives from her side of the family, believed that children must not be exposed to death. They'd be scarred by it. They were Shia Muslims with an overlay of melancholy to their temperaments because of the collective memory of the battle at Karbala and its attendant killings in 680 AD. They knew how to weep, and now they had their own personal reasons for doing so.

It was the 14th of June, 1965, when the first death happened—that of my brother, then thirteen years old. In the dark my mother's eyes looked like black stones. She was quiet then, but my ears have remembered from that time the sound of the lamentation that started later, at first at a low pitch and then louder, which seemed to have been absorbed and retained by the air, so that I could hear it even when no one was crying. It was a language of grief that lost its edge as I grew familiar with it each successive June. The predominant feeling thereafter was one of dread, as though there was more to come. More did come, but not right away. My eyes had their memory too from those days—of car headlights, though we were far from the road, filtering through the bougainvillea creeper beside the front veranda and making patterns on the wall as I lay awake at night on my mattress on the floor in the drawing room, which was cool because of the desert cooler that had been fixed in one of the windows. The house was full of people and everyone slept close together on the floor. My mother said that she had an empty space where her heart had been; my father grew taciturn.

Death for me, at eight years old, meant the black receiver of the dial-up telephone in the drawing room dangling by its cord down the side of the table where it was kept. It had dropped from my mother's hand when she got the news that her son, older than his twin brother by six minutes, had died at my father's sister's place in Sagar, in Madhya Pradesh. The three brothers had gone there to attend a wedding reception—our cousin Prabodh had recently acquired a Polish wife—that happened to fall in the summer vacation. From what I gleaned out of stray conversations between the relatives that had gathered in the house, my brothers, along with their cousins, had gone out for a picnic to a scenic spot by the river and they had decided to go for a swim. No one knew anything for certain. Whatever had happened there seemed to be pure conjecture.

Had my brother Akhil, the older of the twins, drowned while swimming in the Narmada? They were all young, still in their teens, and there was no older person with them who might have taken sensible decisions. His lips had turned blue; had he been bitten by a snake in the water? Did he get cramps while swimming? He'd got a stomach ache. Had it been something to do with his stomach then, indigestion after consuming the difficult to digest baatis that he had never eaten before? Someone said it was 'bund cholera', a quiet form of the disease that did not have any outward manifestation but slowly spread poison in the digestive system. When he complained of a stomach ache again later at night, an older cousin gave him an aspirin. He died the following day with no one any the wiser about what had happened to him. I had not gone to Sagar. I was not told anything about the events, and so, things remained hazy in my head. Whatever little information I had was picked up from hearsay, and questions were not to be asked. My mother who hadn't gone to Sagar either knew more than I did, but the subject had become taboo. I still have no idea what actually took place on that day; perhaps no one did. And if they did, they were certainly not going to discuss whatever little they knew with the children. The one consequence that flowed from those events was that no one from our family ever went to Sagar again, not in all the years that my father's sister lived there, up until much later when her house was sold and the family dispersed to different places. My aunt continued to visit us in Allahabad though, and the incident made no difference to my father's affection for his sister's children. When my father's sister came to our place, she spent all her time lying on a bed in the room that had been set up for her, chewing paan and reading. When she ran through one lot of books, my father would get her another. She'd finished reading all the Hindi books that were already in the house, so my father had more brought in from outside. She had not been untouched by tragedy either. She'd lost in an air crash her eldest son who was training to be a pilot, and in subsequent years, two more sons and her husband. My father who usually had little to say about other people said that she 'had been cheated by life'. In the midst of all this, she never lost her equanimity.

He was dead. His photographs were placed out of sight, shoved into the big metal box with sharp edges in the cupboard in my mother's bedroom. All possible signs of him were wiped out from the house, for everything reminded her of his absence and she could not take it. Perhaps in denial she found a sanctuary from the grief that kept changing form, from disbelief, to anger, to sorrow, but was always present, the elephant in the room that was not supposed to be noticed. For a while, she seemed to have forgotten how to count. When setting out portions of food, for instance, she'd cook and keep out on the dining table for our after-school snack five bowls of kheer or, at other times, bread pudding; but there were only four of us now. The table that had eight straight-backed chairs to go with it was large and made of solid teak, with a top that could be lifted off if the table needed to be moved. Its legs stood in four stone bowls that were filled with water to prevent ants from climbing up to the food. Sometimes she wouldn't notice when there was no water in the bowls, and we would then find ants in the stuff that she had placed on the table. To keep the food safe from ants, especially during the rains, she started putting the after-school snacks inside the white Mena-Lux oven that stood to a side, beside the door of the dining room.

My sister and I, busy playing hopscotch, noughts-and-crosses, or Name-Place-Animal-Thing, caught ourselves laughing and felt guilty. We turned aggressively on friends when they too laughed. I realised then, even though we were too young to think about it coherently, that laughter too is a part of grief—you can laugh and cry simultaneously, for you are not just one person who either laughs or weeps but are composed of several, and one of them may laugh while another grieves, that no moment of laughter or of sorrow is absolute. It was strange how our world kept going when it ought to have stopped. The black bureau in which both the twins kept their things had not been removed from the room. My dead brother's school notebooks covered with brown paper, with his name and the class in which he studied neatly written on them, were still arranged inside it. The mouth organ that had been much coveted and fought over, even though no one could produce from it anything but discordant sound, now lay there forgotten. The box of chocolates that had on it a picture of a ship with complicated sails, which our cousin had brought from Poland, was in the bureau and was now empty. There was the geometry box in which were kept the marbles with which the twins had played when they got home from school, gathering around them other children from the neighbourhood. The marbles rattled as they slid against each other when you picked up the box. I held one up to the light—

the glass was transparent, with a green swirl going through it, and it looked like a small impossible universe.

But even before my brother died, there had been an awareness of death. On our trips to Banaras, we'd see on the road from the railway station to the house, biers carrying the dead—for people came to die in holy Banaras—borne aloft on the shoulders of relatives on their way to the burning ghats of Manikarnika and Harishchandra. The corpses would sometimes be covered with a bright yellow or a pink satin shroud with silver spangles on it, and the funeral procession accompanied by drums and cymbals would turn into a celebration of death, especially if it was an old man who'd died after having lived a long life, or a married woman who had predeceased her husband, for this was considered auspicious. Innocent then of a first-hand experience of death, we would imitate the pall-bearers at home as we strutted about carrying on our shoulders a long stick to stand in for the bier and raise the chant reserved for funeral processions: *Ram Nam Satya Hai!* We'd take for granted that the person who had died was a man and add to the chant a wicked aside, picked up we had no idea where, that the dead son of a bitch was now *mast* or tipsy—*Murda saala mast hai!*

Back at home in Allahabad, we'd lie down on the lawn in front of the house and look at the birds in the sky. My brother Akhil said that the swallow flew the highest, so high that the hawk couldn't get it. It was the only bird that was truly free for it did not die. I don't know where he got this information from, but at the time, it seemed entirely believable, and no one knew of anything else that might refute it. On one of those days, I jumped across my brother's recumbent body as he lay on the grass and later when he died, thought that it was I who had killed him. If you jump over a living person, they stop growing—in other words, they die. Superstitions ruled our lives. The Mirchandani children—Geeta, who always wore frilly frocks, and her neatly shod and dressed brother Suresh—would come over from the house across the road and we'd play games in which we pretended to be dead. In one of them, we'd fall straight from a standing position onto the grass like a dead tree and lie there without stirring for several minutes before scrambling up again. Geeta said that when they went home, they were scolded by their mother for ruining their perfectly ironed 'going out' clothes.

Bilasi, the white-haired kitchen help, had stopped coming, and we found out that she had died. I saw her in a dream; she was smiling, her toothless mouth wide open. Kamla, the sweeper's pretty daughter, had been found dead and lying in a pool of blood near the garden tap under the ashok trees. It was untreated tuberculosis, they said. A girl from class six at school—Madhulika—got malaria, chicken pox and jaundice all at the same time and died. On hot summer nights, we slept on beds fitted with mosquito nets that made them look like strange square ships on the high seas. The beds were set out in a row outside the house on the paved drive in front of the ashok trees. I tried to fall asleep but kept seeing Madhulika's face. In the afternoon, I wandered beneath the trees, plucking and chewing leaves from different ones to find out if any of them had the potential to kill. I didn't die.

But creatures died all the time. There were the squirrels that my brothers killed with their slings; my sister and I went about looking for suitable spots to bury them. There was the dead snake in the garden, with camera-eyes that took a photograph of you if you went near, and its mate came later to wreak vengeance. The book in which we pressed live butterflies during a passing phase in which we thought of ourselves as lepidopterists made a snapping sound when we shut it, and the clouded yellow's wings left a powdery residue on our fingers. The soon-to-die chickens squeezed together in a wire mesh cage outside the butcher's squawked frantically when he caught them by the wings and carried them away; death was in the sudden silence that followed. There were earthworms beneath the soil and caterpillars on the leaves that would soon be eaten by a bird. One life seemed to be contingent on another, continuing only by dint of something else dying. So beneath everything that lived, there was, like a hard diamond, the ineradicable fact of death. The rains brought hordes of flying termites that rushed towards the light and died. Their gossamer wings choked the veranda in the morning and then blew about at the slightest hint of a breeze. But the darkness that they came from seemed to be alive and breathing, with eyes that watched you if you went out alone at night. Sometimes at night a high wind rose and it seemed to fill the earth from end to end with whispering. Then there was silence, like an absence at the heart of the world. Sometimes I'd hear the dull thud of a branch falling in the garden and the wind would start sobbing. The sound, though it was everywhere, seemed to come from the depths of the earth.

1966 arrived. With it came to the house a dreadlocked sadhu who was equipped with a powerful curse. Alms were given to him—atta, rice, fruits, money—but it wasn't enough. Watch out for the fifteenth, he said as he left. Whether it was a coincidence or the power of his curse, my maternal cousin's American wife Jola died on the fifteenth, though it was February and not June. She'd met my cousin Hashim while he was studying in America and they'd fallen in love, married and immediately produced a daughter. Jola, along with their daughter, accompanied him when he returned to India after completing his studies. Things seemed to go well for a while, another child was born, but a few years later, in a morose state of mind, she took an overdose of sleeping pills. She was buried in the Christian cemetery in

Rajapur, and her two children, the daughter aged eleven and the son six, were brought up by their grandmother.

She had died in February but June, too, brought a death. Another cousin, my uncle Amrit Rai's son Amit, had returned in the summer of 1965 from a trek in the Kumaon hills with his brother Alok, my brother Atul, and their friends Muktesh and Pushpesh Pant, looking darker and thinner. Within a few months of coming back, he developed a mysterious pain in his arm that was believed to be due to overexertion at table tennis. However, investigations first in Allahabad and later at the Tata Memorial Hospital in Bombay revealed that he was suffering from acute myeloid leukaemia for which at the time there was no cure. While the tests were being done in Bombay, he wrote to his friends in Allahabad: 'They suspect leukaemia, but surprisingly it affects me as much as would a bout of influenza.' Thereafter, he spent long stretches of time in Bombay, in hospital for blood transfusions, then out of hospital and staying in a flat, waiting till it was time for the next transfusion. There was no knowing when or indeed if he'd be back in Allahabad. Other treatments were tried out. He travelled to Calcutta for homeopathy, which claimed to have a cure. There was some talk of his being taken to the United States. He was given injections of liver extract recommended by a Baba. Various treatments were tried out. Nothing worked. In the second half of May, he wrote to his maternal aunt and uncle about the superstitions he had started creating around his illness. If, he told himself, his parents arrived at the hospital in an old taxi, he would come through it all—the sickness, the transfusions, the injections; if not, then .... He wrote about how, when his parents came, he did not have the courage to look out of the window to see which car they had come in. He died in Bombay on 21 June 1966, twenty-one days after he had turned eighteen.

It was several decades after his death that he became more real for me than when he had been alive. Now and then I tried to recall him, but it was no use. I could not even dredge up an image of what he had looked like. I remembered him at an ice-cream party that was held on the lawn of our Drummond Road house. Every summer there'd be a couple of ice-cream parties. The hand-crank ice-cream maker was a wooden bucket that was filled with ice and rock salt, into which was lowered a metal canister that connected with a cranking handle, and in the canister were the ice-cream ingredients. The handle needed to be cranked continuously for the ice-cream to set. Everyone had a go at the handle that turned easily at first and then needed more force to be applied to it as the ice-cream began to harden. We fooled around while waiting for the ice-cream to be ready. One memory I had from that day was of my cousin giving me a shoulder-ride. It wasn't much of a memory and I still could not remember his face. There were no photographs of him to fall back on, for, as had happened with my mother when her son, my brother Akhil, died, Amit's photos too had been hidden away from his mother. There was one of him wearing short trousers and a full-sleeved shirt that had stood in a frame on the table in his mother's room, but it disappeared after he died. And we had none at our place. Neither my parents, nor my brother Atul, who was only a year younger than Amit and old enough to travel alone, had gone to see him during the months that he was in Bombay. No letters were written to him or received. Perhaps this detachment could be put down to my parents not having been able to get over the death of their own son which, after all, had happened less than a year ago.

Six years after Amit died, Arvind Krishna Mehrotra, who had been one of his closest friends, put together a manuscript of all of Amit's writing that he could lay his hands on. Both of them had started writing poems early. Arvind then lived next door to the Rais at 20 Hastings Road, with only a low boundary wall separating the two houses, and it was across this wall that Amit and he had exchanged their poems. The material collected by Arvind included some poems, a couple of stories and a play, an incomplete journal, and some of the letters that Amit had written to various people from Bombay. It was when I saw this still unpublished manuscript—*All to Remember*—that I realised how gifted my cousin had been. Most of the poems had been written in the one inspired year from September 1964 to October 1965. A long untitled poem, clairvoyant in its clear-sightedness, ended with:

> At last I knew my time was come
> (To quote an ancient phrase)
> For a moment
> I understood
> Understood for a brief
> A hasty moment
> Paralysed to Eternity
> The terrible slavery of the bow to its string.

In another poem called 'When I Stray', he wrote:

> When I stray into the penumbra of feeling
> Each clump I see
> Is a painful memory
> And the ground
> Ever on the other side
> My joy
> I try and rise above it all
> But what am I after all—
> A ragged feather on a vast mosaic.

Or, in 'Musings for a Paratrooper':

> dead.
> Dead ... can you imagine
> eyelids that won't blink
> when the raindrops
> drop on them ...

My cousins Amit and Alok Rai, along with Arvind, had also, in September 1965, on the pattern of the New York little magazines, especially *fuck you/a magazine of the arts,* started their own mimeographed magazine in Allahabad: *damn you/a magazine of the arts.* The first issue, which consisted of some sheets of paper tied together loosely with a piece of string, carried poems by the three editors, and it was their first appearance in print. The second issue of *damn you* appeared in March 1966, with the anonymous editorial statement written by Amit who was then back in Allahabad, the cancer briefly in remission. There were to be four more issues of the magazine and Amit's name appeared in all six, even though he'd died weeks after the second issue appeared.

When Amit died, my mother expressed her regret at having envied his mother, both of whose sons were alive when one of hers was dead; she had cast her black eye on them, she said. My aunt, Amit's mother, remembered the astrologer who'd predicted that her son would have a short life. Years later, my mother spoke of how, to make sense of the events, they had all come to believe in the stars and that the stars had foretold tragedy. For me those years are coloured a dull ochre, the red ochre of old blood that I have come to associate with death and mourning.

A few months before my mother died in 1993, I came into her room one day to find her sitting before the cupboard built into the wall with both of its doors open. She was tearing up letters. In the cupboard, there was a leather folder that bore the picture of an eagle and it was stuffed with letters. Most of them were written in Urdu on blue paper and the few written on white had turned yellow. She'd take a look at each letter before tearing it with a ripping sound and throwing it on the ground, which was now a mess of scattered, torn paper. It looked like a scene of carnage. The letters were all written by her brother from overseas. At the time of Partition, intimidated by the violence that he saw around him, he had taken the decision of moving to Pakistan with his Hindu wife and two young sons. His wife Kamla belonged to Dehradun and they had met at the University of Allahabad where they were both studying. He deeply regretted the move to Pakistan almost from the day he arrived in Karachi and he was soon looking for ways to get out of there.

An opportunity presented itself when he got employed by the UN in the Pakistan quota and left for his first posting in New York. He'd visit from there once in a few years, bearing gifts—records, chocolates, perfumes, and clothes that we, unaware of current trends in fashion, found strange and never wore. He'd also send pictures from New York; in one of them, he stood in a snow-covered street wearing an overcoat and holding the hand of his daughter who'd been born in Karachi and was then eight or nine years old. And he wrote letters full of nostalgia, some of which were in the box in my mother's cupboard and that she was now intent on tearing. From New York he moved to Beirut, and wrote letters in which he missed the early morning ruckus of the thousands of sparrows that lived in the madhumalti creeper in the courtyard of the Nawab-ki-Deorhi house in Banaras. Then the news came in June 1968 that he had died of a cardiac arrest. I visited his wife, my aunt Kamla, in 1983, in Geneva, where she now lived with her daughter and sons, one of whom was in the

International Labour Organization. Every night before going to bed, she'd light a candle to remember her husband, now dead for fifteen years.

When I visited Faatmaan in 1994, a few months after the deaths of my mother and my aunt, I found their graves as well as that of my grandmother. Other relatives, too, were buried there, including my grandfather Mirza Mohammad Mahmood. But my uncle Mirza Mohammad Taqi was not where he should have been, with the rest of the family. He had been buried in Beirut where he died. I thought of the missing grave and wondered whether it still existed in Beirut, a city that had again and again seen turbulent times. It must have been destroyed, I thought, during those periods of prolonged unrest.

But before my uncle's death in 1968 that had occurred by an odd coincidence on 21 June, the same date as my cousin Amit's in 1966, there had also been my great-grandmother Ummatuz Zahra's death at Nawab-ki-Deorhi in June 1967. Her death was little noticed or mourned because she was by then in her mid-nineties and was expected to die. For years she'd been lying on a string cot in the little passageway that led from the front of the house to the courtyard at the back, positioned in such a way that it caught the current of air that passed between the two open spaces. The passageway had doors at both ends, which, when closed, converted the space into a small room that stayed cool in summer. At other times, on days when the sun was out in winter, she'd be moved to the stone-front veranda. She was unable to walk and it was unclear whether this was due to old age or because her hip, broken after a fall, had been wrongly set. There was no one left in the house, who could now be asked to clear the confusion. In her time, she'd been an inventive cook, reputed in the family for her very large, almost translucent, paper-thin chapattis. But by the time I saw her, she was no longer mobile. She'd lie, small and white-haired, on her sagging charpoy that had a pot-sized hole cut into the rope-work the bed was composed of, the strings tightly wound and smooth around the edges of the opening, beneath which a chamber pot would be placed when she needed to urinate. I didn't know quite how the arrangement worked, she must have had someone to help her, but I once saw the charpoy with the mattress removed and the hole exposed when she had been taken for a bath. Most of the day she'd chew away with her gums at the paan that was pounded in a little brass mortar-and-pestle set before being given to her, for she had no teeth. There was a bell metal spittoon placed beside the bed, which would be brought up close to her face so that she could spit out the paan into it. She had retained even in extreme age an opium addiction, though the afeem had shrunk in quantity to a tiny ball, which she took along with her paan. It made her voluble, and she'd talk about things that belonged to another time and that no one could make sense of. Her skin, criss-crossed with wrinkles, folded over her cheeks like a soft handkerchief, and the holes in her earlobes had become elongated with the weight of the heavy earrings that she must have worn for most of her life. If you gently pulled at them, they opened up like little windows.

She wasn't in the veranda when I visited the house again, and there was no sign of her string cot either in the room at the end of the courtyard where all the furniture no longer in use was stored. It must have been given away after she died.

The House of Fiction

> When one is endowed with imagination, as you are, one possesses all the landscapes one has loved, and this is the inalienable treasure of the heart. But really a home where you have memories of your family, a home which you cannot see except through reveries which recede into the distant past, is a very moving thing.
>
> Marcel Proust, *Letters to the Lady Upstairs*

Near the high boundary wall of my mother's ancestral home in Banaras was a tall silk-cotton tree that blossomed in March, splashing the sky with blood red. The large fleshy blooms with their five petals would lie on the ground beneath the tree and we used them to engage in mock fights. My sister and I each picked up a flower and, foes until death, entangled in battle one of the anthers on the stamens of our respective flowers. Whoever succeeded in decapitating the other's emerged the winner. The match was short and savage, the tender anthers tore off easily, and we soon tired of the game. Next to the silk-cotton was a grove of wild bananas in which djinns were said to live. They looked like ordinary folk, and Halima who worked as a cook for my grandmother had seen them moving about in long white kurtas, but when she went close, they disappeared into the well beside the grove. It was an old well and from it seemed to emanate a mist thick with tales of suicide and tragedy. When you looked into the well, you could see, beyond the mossy green edges, water that glinted like black ink far in the depths. It beckoned, and exercising a kind of hypnosis, invited you to leap in. We'd throw pebbles into the well to see how long they would take to reach the water, and they kept falling, never making the splashing sound we were waiting to hear. We called into the well and the echo of our voices, rounded and hollow, was thrown back at us.

Beyond the banana grove was a stretch of land with a few guava trees to one side and a tall Java plum from which, in the rains, dropped the small ripe dark purple fruit. Beside the Java plum was a rundown building that had a terracotta roof black with age and falling to pieces, with many of the tiles missing. The building had been let to a tenant by the name of Izhar who was notable for his many children and his many hens. The children, snotty nosed and tangle haired, their mouths ringed with purple from the plums, played in the bare yard outside the building, looking so like each other as to be interchangeable. There was a rickety wire-mesh coop in which the hens lived. They could be seen pecking at bits of dal and rice in the little drain that always had remnants of food from the utensils that had been washed at the hand-pump beside it. When anyone dropped by, there was no need for a call-bell as Izhar's hens would set up a vigorous squawking, and a similar goodbye ceremony took place when the visitors left. Whenever we visited, the hens made a loud announcement for us too.

Throughout the sixties, during my childhood and early teenage, my mother, my siblings and I travelled from Allahabad to Banaras at least twice every year. Usually, we took a train on the small gauge from Rambagh station that rattled along, blowing soot and smoke in our faces. It stopped at every sleepy little station on the way, and even where a stop was not scheduled, there was always someone on the train ready to stop it by pulling the chain. Depending on the hour, there were milkmen who got on with clanking milk-cans or students who carried their bicycles into the train to effect more speedy arrival and departure. This was the time when major events were taking place—India fought with China in 1962 and lost, Nehru died two years later, the Americans did terrible things in Vietnam and the war went on interminably, Martin Luther King was assassinated, but we kept always moving from Allahabad to Banaras and back, as though caught in suspended motion on our train, the speed of which was affected by nothing. There was a similarity among the stations we passed, for nearly all of them had a peepul or a banyan tree with a sadhu sitting beneath it, and the image repeated so often was like a tableau that moved with the train from station to station. The names of the stations carried a peculiar resonance, and I rolled them on my tongue like a connoisseur tasting wine: Handia, Jangiganj, Kachhwa Road, Aurai, Madhosingh, Raja Talab, Manduadih. They had about them something delicious, reminiscent of wet earth and samosas.

The house was in Lohatia, the ironmongers' quarter. It was a crowded part of the city, though much of the city was crowded. You started out from the station, seated precariously on a rickshaw with its high, narrow seat sloping forward, and held on tight to the small rexine-coated wooden armrests as the rickshaw picked up speed, seeming to pass through the whole town, the bazaars and the houses leaning at improbable angles, though Lohatia, located in Ausanganj, was not so far from the station. You finally came to the cobbled Sant Kabir Road that led to the ironmongers' quarter. The dark stones of the road, smooth and shiny with use, seemed to be made of iron too. The road was busy at all times of the day, leading past Kabir Chaura and two government hospitals to the Town Hall and beyond. But much before the Town Hall, a narrow gali branched off to the left and then took another sharp left, becoming the kutcha pebble-strewn alley that led to Nawab-ki-Deorhi. On one side of the lane were shops where ironsmiths worked hard for much of the day, banging metal on metal. Woks and cauldrons of humungous size, chains and saws and axes, bird cages and mousetraps, horseshoes and nails, kitchen tongs, sieves and iron ladles, spades and hoes, and watering cans—there wasn't much that was not made in those little shops. The air seemed to be torn to shreds by crashing and hammering sounds which mysteriously vanished once you entered the tall black gate. And there you'd see it, that white elephant of a house, for it was emptied now of most of its inhabitants, with its pillars and verandas, the walls colonised by vines, but still standing on tottering feet, ready for the day that couldn't be far when it would meet the dust it had been raised from.

My grandmother and my aunt lived in the portion of the haveli that had once been called the chhota mahal. Along with the bada mahal, a row of garages whose high, black corrugated tin doors were always shut, and a couple of shops giving on to the busy lane, it was part of the complex known as Nawab-ki-Deorhi. The structure was built with a combination of stone and thin *lakhori* or burnt clay bricks that suggested age, though it was not clear how old the house was. It had been bought by my mother's great-grandfather Rai Narsingh Das at some point in the last quarter of the nineteenth century, but since the house already existed then, it would have been a good deal older. Recently I received an email from one Syed Nazre Ali Khan 'Fraz', who suspected that his ancestors had inhabited the same haveli, possibly even owned it. Over a few emails in which we pieced together the details of his family, we concluded that his ancestors had probably lived in the same haveli in the 1790s. 'An old thing,' he called it, going back at least to the mid-eighteenth century. A tortuous line of ancestry, the resounding names no less tortuous, connected him to Nawab-ki-Deorhi. From what I learnt, Nawab Azeez-ul-Mulk Ameen-ud-Daulah Khan Bahadur Syed Ali Ibrahim Khan Naser Jung 'Khaleel', the nephew of Syed Nazre's great-grandfather Nawab Wahshat-Qalam Khan Bahadur Haji Syed Ahmad Ali Khan 'Qayamat' of Azeemabad (Patna in the eighteenth-century), was posted in Banaras as the chief magistrate in the year 1781 and was later appointed the subedar. Subsequently he became the governor of the Banaras State. He was said to have lived in a haveli in Nawab-ki-Deorhi and his family continued to live there even after his death in 1793–94. If the haveli he lived in was indeed the same one, then Rai Narsingh Das must have bought the place from his descendants.

There was no portrait of Rai Narsingh Das in the house, which added to the air of mystery that hung about him. He had been born in 1832 and belonged to the same affluent mercantile family of Agarwal banias of Banaras that later, in 1850, also produced the pioneering Hindi litterateur Bhartendu Harishchandra. Of his ancestors, only the names from the tangled family tree remain—Lala Hanuman Prasad, Rai Ram Pratap, Rai Shyam Das, Rai Ishwari Das, Rai Tara Chand, Rai Kamal Nayan, Raja Indramani, Rai Beugali Nath, Raja Khayaliram, and in the next generation—Rai Rakshi Ram, the father of Raja Patnimal Bahadur (1770–1844) and Rai Sri Krishna (1787–1818), the latter's son, who in turn had four sons of his own—Rai Narottam Das, Rai Narayan Das, Rai Narsingh Das, and the youngest, Rai Hari Das, dead at the age of twelve. All of it is a rather confusing hotchpotch, the dates unreliable with the sons being born long after the recorded death of the father and no mention of the daughters. What we do know, from family hearsay, is that the seventeenth-century ancestors were diwans in the Moghal administration and later under the East India Company, controlling vast jagirs in Central and West Bihar. While the rest of the family settled in Allahabad or Patna, Patnimal Bahadur moved to Banaras, and that is how the story of my mother's ancestors began in that city. Rai Narsingh Das, even though he lived for most of his life in Banaras, owned in Allahabad property that he had either inherited or acquired, said to be no less than thirty-five bungalows. It was in Allahabad that he died when his landau met with an accident in 1901, and that is where he is buried.

I recently decided to visit his grave. There is a Shia graveyard in Karbala, a locality named after the place in present day Iraq where Imam Husain and his family were martyred. Karbala is located in the area called Chakia, which is far from where I live, though no distance within Allahabad is very great. However, as soon as my nephew and I set out, we came upon a roadblock outside the Allahabad High Court. There was a sea of lawyers in black coats out on the road, looking like some indestructible form of life, standing so close together that it was impossible to get past. They were on strike, demanding that the Uttar Pradesh Service Tribunal Act 2021 function from Allahabad rather than from Lucknow. Once we were past that hurdle, in a matter of minutes we were at Karbala. My nephew pointed out the grave to me. It was raised on a platform and made entirely of marble, with a headstone which stated that Mirza Ghulam Hyder alias Rai Narsingh Das, the 'Raees-e-Azam' of Banaras, had come to grief in Allahabad. There was a border of roses intertwined with leaves carved along the sides of the grave and an inscription in Farsi on its upper edge. When I saw the grave, the figure that had hovered, phantom-like, over the history of my mother's family became real for me at last.

Rai Narsingh Das already had a Hindu wife, said to be the paternal aunt of Bhartendu, and two children, Rai Prahlad Das (1857–1904) and Rani Bibi (dates unknown). It seemed to be a peaceful homely sort of life. Not for long, though. Things changed when he met a Shia woman, and the story went that he fell in love with the exquisite paans prepared by her. His Hindu family was of the opinion that the woman, Amir Begum, was a courtesan who had ensnared him with her coquettish ways. He converted to Shia Islam presumably to marry her and took the name of Ghulam Hyder, though he was generally known as Babba Huzoor. He soon had a Muslim family alongside the Hindu one that he had moved away from, and seemed to embody in his person the streams of the two cultures. The story that was passed down in the Muslim half of the family was that he had fallen in love with Shia Islam and not with the courtesan; in fact, there was no evidence that Amir Begum was a courtesan in the first place. But then, there was the mystery of where, if she wasn't a courtesan, he could have met her in those days of purdah when women did not appear before strangers. It was too late to find out. The progeny from his two wives continued to meet each other in later generations. Rai Krishna Das (1892–1980), the son of Rai Prahlad Das and a contemporary of Premchand, also wrote stories and songs. In 1920, with the donation of his personal collection of art objects, he set up the Bharat Kala Bhavan, the museum in Banaras which his son Rai Anand Krishna continued to run in the capacity of director.

With his Muslim wife, Babba Huzoor had three daughters, Mariam Begum, Malka Begum and Kulsoom Begum, and one son, Mirza Kazim Hussain. Malka Begum married one Agha Asghar Ali and had a daughter by the name of Ummatuz

Zahra, who subsequently became my great-grandmother, though it was only much later that I came to know her name. Mirza Kazim Hussain married first one Mehdi Begum, but for reasons unknown, the marriage was a non-starter, and he went on to marry Abbasi Begum with whom he had three boys, Mirza Mohammad Mahmood, Mirza Mohammad Masood and Mirza Mohammad Dawood. Ummatuz Zahra, when she reached puberty, was married, a little confusingly, to Nawab Asghar Quli of Bhikna Pahadi near Patna, whose ancestors were believed to have come from Iran. So, were Ummatuz Zahra's father and her husband both called Asghar? It could have been that a name once erroneously written into the family tree was then instated there for good. There was no one left who could be asked. I remember well my great-grandmother Ummatuz Zahra. By the time I came to know her, she was around ninety years old. She would lie all day on a sagging charpoy in the stone-front veranda, wearing a dark petticoat and a high-necked cotton blouse that had buttons down the front. I never saw her standing up.

I didn't find out the circumstances that made her shift to Nawab-ki-Deorhi from Bhikna Pahadi. Not only was she in Nawab-ki-Deorhi but her husband was there as well. I have no memory of him, but he was said to have been a gentle sage of a man, who lived in a room in the garden with his Persian cat, a mynah and a bad-tempered parrot that shrieked abuses in a distinctive Shia vocabulary. There was the story about Nawab Asghar Quli that he'd lie on a chaise-longue in the garden in an opium-induced sleep, and sparrows would suss out his profuse white curls to build a nest. Once every week, he'd put on an Aligarhi pyjama and achkan, part his long hair down the middle and go to the bazaar to buy opium. There seemed to have been no concern about where the money to live would come from, though it may have been money worries that brought them to Nawab-ki-Deorhi in the first place.

The immediate connection with Nawab-ki-Deorhi now was Ummatuz Zahra's daughter, my grandmother Munawwari Begum who, at the age of twelve, had been married to Mirza Kazim Hussain's son, her uncle Mirza Mohammad Mahmood. My grandfather, considerably senior to his wife, died before I was born, but there was a picture of him, a bald man with a kindly expression on his face, sitting barefooted on a cane chair. Munawwari Begum, who by her own calculation of dates was born in 1894, must then have been married in 1906. Newly arrived from Bhikna Pahadi, she could ride a horse and was fond of flying kites. Of course, there was no one now who knew what she was like then.

I remember her from the 1960s, by which time she had developed an imperious manner and a caustic tongue. She looked like a species of snow eagle with her white hair gathered into a bun at the nape of her neck, her aquiline nose and, behind her glasses, her sharp astute eyes. She had a biting sense of humour and her rather picturesque speech quickly travelled between the contrasting landscapes of an unpolluted, refined Urdu and the most uninhibited and coarse abuses. Once, on being asked by the cook whether she liked the taro root curry that had been cooked specially for her, she replied a little enigmatically, 'It was looking at me very attentively.' The puzzled cook wondered what she could possibly have meant till my aunt, who understood better her mother's cryptic speech, deciphered it for her that there wasn't enough turmeric in the curry, so that the pieces of taro, too white, looked like staring eyes.

Mirza Mohammad Mahmood and Munawwari Begum lived on in the chhota mahal, but not much is known about Kazim Hussain's other two sons Dawood and Masood. Abbasi Begum had died in childbirth, leaving Mirza Kazim heartbroken. Babba Huzoor thought that the most effective panacea for his son's grief would be to send him to England to study law. There is a photograph of him in a tweed coat and tie, a cane in his hand, walking on an English street; the date on its back is 1875. But how could he have been in England in 1875? He would have been around twenty then, for his father had only been born in 1832, but he looked older in the photograph. There is certainly some confusion regarding dates; they don't match. But give or take a couple of decades, what might Mirza Kazim have seen when he arrived in England? City streets would have echoed with the din of horse-drawn traffic—cabriolets, omnibuses and hackney coaches clattering past on cobblestones—with romance in the air and many entertainments on offer. There'd have been theatres, pleasure gardens and shops displaying the latest fashions—plenty, in fact, to distract him from his grief. He soon fell in love with an English cleric's daughter. They married and he brought her to India where he served as a state minister to the Nawab of Rampur. He stayed there for several years before returning to Nawab-ki-Deorhi where his mother had meanwhile been looking after his three young sons. He now asked his new wife to teach the boys English manners and conversation, and after a few lessons, Masood had learnt enough English to be able to complain to his step-mother, '*Dawood haramzada khilao-ed the anda to the kauvah.*' (Dawood the bastard fed the egg to the crow.)

It didn't take Mirza Kazim long to develop acrimonious relations with his mother. He sold the house for a song and again left for England where he was last heard of in Kent. His mother, after some struggle, managed to get back the house. There was no picture of Babba Huzoor in the house, but Mirza Kazim, in shervani and Kashmiri cap, leaned across, disconcertingly life-sized, from his portrait that was suspended at an angle above the sofa in the sehenchi, the anteroom attached to the bada kamra, which, as its name made clear, was a large room, with a stone floor, arches and niches, adjacent to the courtyard. The whitewashed wall of the room had developed damp patches that looked like strange animals walking across it. Fungus and moisture had left their impact on his portrait too and the lower part of it was ruined, but the face was untouched. There were other pictures of Kazim Hussain in the drawing room, gently fading behind their glass frames, though none of Abbasi Begum.

There was one picture with his later wife, the British priest's daughter whose name has slipped into oblivion. Their son Horace was a young lad in one of the pictures and in another, the daughter Eunice, who died at the age of thirteen, dressed in lehenga and blouse. The past overwhelmed the present, with its photographs of the dead, more numerous than those of the living. On the wall facing Mirza Kazim Hussain's portrait in the sehenchi was another portrait hanging at eye level in a silver frame, all billows and whorls, of a rather Junoesque woman with a mysterious smile and brown hair falling on her alabaster white shoulders. She met your eyes steadily, as though trying to reveal with her intimate gaze the secret of who she was. She belonged not on this wall but perhaps in a gallery of portraits painted by Charles Joshua Chaplin whose *Belle Femme en Déshabillé: Nineteenth Century French Portrait of a Young Society Beauty* I came across while trying to find the forgotten portrait online. But the woman in the portrait I remembered had been more curvaceous than the one painted by Chaplin.

The chhota mahal, located at the end of a considerable portion of land, was whitewashed with dark patches where the lime had flaked off. When you approached it from the gate, you first came to a long stone-flagged veranda that had a ceiling with black wooden beams running horizontally across it. An old jasmine creeper with a thick coiled trunk partly covered the veranda, and at night, a bulb under an aluminum shade burned beneath the delicate leaves. The veranda ended on one side in an arch beyond which was a poorly lighted toilet. There was a washroom at the other end of the veranda too, with a floor of red cement on which a thin stream of water constantly dripped from a defective tap, creating perpetual damp on the walls. Just outside the washroom was a low water trough inhabited by various forms of algae. There was a narrow wooden door beside the washroom, which was fastened with an iron chain that nested on a hook embedded there for the purpose. This was the side entrance to the house. It was used more frequently than the big main gate, though it was too narrow for rickshaws and cars, which had to stop outside.

Doors, each folding back and becoming two narrow doors, led off from the veranda into a row of four rooms of different sizes, two of which opened onto a square courtyard. The dining room, the third of the four, had three framed prints of scenes from the Scottish Highlands—moors purple with heather, lumbering beasts with pointy horns and shaggy coats, the sun breaking through lowering skies over a loch—that hung above an old-fashioned dresser made of dark teak that was used for keeping cups and saucers, sugar and tea. There were two intriguing little passageways beside the two middle rooms, also equipped with doors that connected the front veranda to the courtyard, but these rooms had several doors which opened into the courtyard anyway. The passages were used like rooms, and I remember bags of cement stored there when the renovation of one of the rooms was taking place. My great-grandmother

Ummatuz Zahra, when she was very old and immobile, would lie in one of the passage-rooms. The space which, in the hot summer months, caught a current of air remained cool. In the late 1960s, when the house finally got a telephone, the black instrument with its silver dial and clunky receiver sat on a tall narrow chiffonier in the first of the passages, its shrill ring screaming throughout the house when someone called. The telephone was an object of much wonder, and Halima, who picked up the calls that my mother made from Allahabad would shout at the top of her voice into the receiver, all the better to help it travel the long way it had to go.

One of the two middle rooms of the four was my grandmother's. Most of the room was occupied by two low takhts that had been joined together to form one very large bed that could fit four or five people. We'd all crowd up on the bed to listen to the stories that my grandmother told us late into the night. We followed her textured voice as though into the depths of an enchanted labyrinth. The stories were often 'tota-maina' tales, in which the entire action was narrated in the form of a conversation between a parrot and a mynah about the human follies that they were witness to. The dramatis personae were usually shahzadis and shahzadas who found themselves caught in imbroglios from which they were saved in the nick of time by the cunning manoeuvres of the fisherman or the bird-catcher who happened to be with them. Our favourite story was the one about the eponymous afeemchi whose failure to kick his opium addiction landed him in all sorts of tricky situations and provided fodder for infinite mirth. She would start telling the story with a straight face but would soon be shaking with laughter as she narrated the misadventures of the perpetually sleep-addled afeemchi.

It is her resonant voice that I remember filling the grey sky of dawn as she recited verses in Arabic from the Quran. She learnt Nagari at the age of seventy-five in order to be able to read the Ramayana and the Mahabharata. She told us with amused disbelief about Abhimanyu, Arjuna's son, who, in the version of the Mahabharata that she was reading, had heard while he was in his mother's womb, the secret of how to enter the chakravyuha, which was the lethal defence formation used by the Kauravas against the Pandavas, but missed the strategy for exit. But then, she was easily amused—the noise of stomping feet coming from the sehenchi as one of my cousins took a lesson in Bharatanatyam sounded, she said with a mischievous smile, like 'a camel that's run amok, being tamed'. She loved the playful and linguistically agile riddles invented by Amir Khusro and she'd often quiz us with these, refusing to reveal the answers till we'd had enough time to think of them on our own and had failed.

From my grandmother's room, through the door framed by madhumalti, you could see at the southern end of the courtyard two tall Chinese fan palms on the sides of two steps with a raised pattern of arches carved into their stonework. On hot summer afternoons, when the loo gathered force, whipping through the palms, you could hear the dry fronds rattling. The steps led up to a veranda elevated above the courtyard. It opened into the bada kamra, which had doors with panes of coloured glass underneath fluted arches and anterooms on both sides of it. The courtyard had rooms on three sides of it and another long veranda on the northern side, set with Italian tiles in black, white and ochre, with floral tiles forming the border. The veranda had hanging lights, never switched on, in old-fashioned shades made of glass in different colours. A large mirror hung on the wall at the end of the veranda, multiplying the tiles and creating an illusion of distance. This veranda led into the imambara.

What was missing in the courtyard was a fountain. Instead, there was a tap placed at a height within a small cement enclosure that released a dismal stream of water. Along the western wall of the courtyard and opening into it, were four rooms, one of them fitted up as a drawing room with a sofa and three chairs upholstered in pale blue cretonne. I never saw anyone sitting on them, though at some point, the room had been used to entertain guests. This furniture now had an unused look. We would jump up and down on the plump sofa, for the springs were still good. There was an old wind-up His Master's Voice gramophone on a low table along with a stack of vinyl records and a small yellow box with 'Twin Steel Needles approximately 200' written on it and a logo of the manufacturers, The Twins, in which the letters were intertwined with a tiny drawing of the twins. A small screw allowed a needle to be fitted on to the stylus which rested on the grooves in the record and produced sound. The records were old and the same needles were used again and again, making the sound warped and scratchy, but we still played them, especially the one at the end of which, the singer, as if quickly trying to get on to the 'sound-train' before it left, that is, before the record ended, said in a high-pitched breathless voice, '*Mera naam Janki Bai Ilahabadi!*' We listened till the end, waiting for her to say her name, for it seemed then as if she had come out of the record and was right there in the room.

From inside the third room on this western side of the courtyard three steps led up to a fourth room, which was completely dark even during the day. The little light that entered from the door only served to reveal forlorn things—chairs with legs missing, a bed with broken springs, a stone mortar-and-pestle, the top of a stone hand-mill with the bottom missing, a fan without wings—objects like lost souls adrift in a world that no longer had any use for them. The room was not in much use, but the discarded stuff in it was pushed aside and beds with sparkling white sheets were set up in it in summer. It was cool in there even without a fan on long June days when the loo blowing outside withered whatever came in its path. My mother and aunt would lie in this room, talking in low voices in a code language that we kids could not decipher, in which the sibilant sound of 's' and the feathery one of 'f' recurred time and again, bringing to mind the whispering of the wind passing through the trees. The rising and falling cadence was strangely soothing, all the more for being quite devoid of meaning. The 'dark room' as it was called, ever since the time it had been used for developing photographs by an amateur photographer in the family, opened into a large draughty bathroom that was cold in winter. The bathroom had a Victorian look, with a big mirror that had turned blind over time, reflecting blurry images inside a frame placed above a wash stand with discoloured brass taps shaped like four-petalled flowers. The taps often let out a hiss of air instead of water. There was a tall window with vertical iron bars set high up on the wall outside which was a busy gali. Nothing could be seen from the window, except the tops of the match-box-like houses on the other side of the gali that had been painted in blues, yellows and white, but were now encrusted with black moss that had spread on them like a skin disease. Sounds travelled up from the lane. Every day the vegetable seller went past around noon, shouting in a singsong voice—*soya methi gobhi gajar mooli! tamatar aloo baigan lauki!* His stock of vegetables, by no means small, seemed always to be the same when we went there in winter. Sometimes you heard snatches of conversation in Bhojpuri that entered my ears and flowed into what I did not recognise then as a sleeping pool of languages within me.

The imambara was a long narrow room with stone pillars and five green doors beneath fluted arches. The doors had wooden louvres, but they were fixed and did not open. The central area in the room was occupied by an ornate wooden replica of the grave of Imam Hussain, the grandson of Prophet Mohammad, and on a low table beside it were holy books with frayed printed covers of thick paper. Against the wall stood some standards and banners decorated with silver and gold embroidery, representing the ones carried to the battlefield at Karbala in 680 AD. Chandeliers of various sizes swung down on chains from the rather low ceiling, the largest, central one fussy with complicated bulbs, its glass yellow with age and lack of use, imparting a grand aura that compensated for the absence of light. The stone-flagged floor of the imambara felt cool under the feet and the room smelt of incense and dried roses.

My grandmother, a stickler for religious ritual, held a majlis there every Thursday and expected everyone to attend it. She read out in a high voice about the tragedy of Karbala. The Urdu interspersed with Arabic became a barrier to understanding for me, not that I was particularly attentive. It was much more fun to see which of the pious old ladies at the majlis slept through it all, and which ones displayed a talent for weeping convincingly at the right moments. Then there was the sweet sherbet, consecrated beforehand by my grandmother. When the majlis was over, she spooned it into our mouths from a small embossed bowl of beaten silver, two teaspoons into each mouth. This was something to be looked forward to, not for the sherbet itself that was sweet and quite without flavour, but because it meant that we could finally get up from the durree on the hard floor.

There was a majlis every day during Muharram, at which the Shia community of Banaras gathered, and food was cooked in vast quantities. Physically strong, my grandmother was able to single-handedly lift off the fire cauldrons heavy with food for the many people who were present at mealtimes. Looking at her, it would have been hard to believe that Indian women were the frail dominated creatures that people imagined them to be. When she became too old to handle the job, a helper had to be hired. On certain days, groups of mourners or anjumans would arrive to recite nohas and marsiyas, which would be followed by matam, chest-beating that was a display of devotion to Imam Hussain and a remembrance of his suffering. Matam sometimes took an extreme form when some of the more devout men lacerated themselves with chains and knives in a frenzy of passion, though this usually happened when they were outside, in the gali, and I never saw them do it. The orange sky of those Muharram evenings seemed to echo the melancholy that would settle on the house. Among the things you heard about Muharram, one was that a Brahmani anjuman composed of Hindu women used to come to the imambara. There is no sign of them now and there are none left who remember them. The present times encourage dyeing in a single colour the myriad threads that were woven into the tapestry of religious belief.

Adjacent to the imambara, a small passage led to the waiting hall, which was a dark narrow room at one end of which was a flight of stairs that went up to the roof, each stone step about a foot high. The waiting hall had been, in earlier times, a reception room for visitors, but now was mostly locked up. It had on the far side a door with broken panes, outside which was a porch with crumbling pillars that shed a powdery white dust. Formal visitors had waited in this room opening on to the porch, after having sent word inside of their arrival. But there were no such visitors now and the porch looked abandoned, with not many cars or rickshaws stopping there. On hot summer nights, the servants spread out their bedding in the porch. There was a large raised platform right in front of the porch, and if you climbed up the steps, you came to another well. The well was covered up after rats burrowed into the walls and created a maze of passages through which foul water from the underground sewers started to seep into the water in the well.

Beyond the porch was the entrance to the bada mahal, a tall sturdy door of heavy wood beneath a fluted arch. On the external lime-washed wall of the bada mahal was repeated the pattern of the ubiquitous fluted arch. A single bulb at night illuminated a small area outside the bada mahal with an arc of sickly yellow light. Inside the bada mahal was a courtyard similar to but larger than the one in the chhota mahal, with rooms around it on all four sides and an imambara of its own. There had been an upper storey of rooms too, taken down when the worn-out walls started collapsing and created a safety hazard. There was a door on the roof of the chhota mahal that used to open into these upper storey rooms of the bada mahal. But with the rooms that it led to long gone, this door was now locked. This was the door through which my maternal uncle had conducted a love affair with his cousin Raazia, who lived on the other side of it in the bada mahal. She died of tuberculosis when she was eighteen, and the blossoming love was nipped in the bud. We seldom went to the bada mahal, but it was where Rai Narsingh Das, the patriarch of the family had lived. Belying its name, this part of the haveli, with the land attached to it sold many years ago, seemed to be smaller and more rundown than the chhota mahal, and it was clear that its days of splendour were past. No one remembered which room Rai Narsingh Das had lived in. The only thing that remained of him now was his two-metre-long turban of watermelon-pink silk that had ornamental motifs embroidered on it with gold zari. Stitched onto a quilt, it had been preserved by my mother's cousin Alia Begum, who presented it to me solemnly, as though passing on something as significant as the Olympic flame, which must never be allowed to go out. She had been a custodian of history for the better part of a century, but history too is finite. The threads of the silk had become frayed, eaten away here and there by silverfish.

Mariam Begum's husband has been forgotten, for the marriage did not work out and the couple went their separate ways, but only after they had produced two children, Anwarul Hasan and Nazneen Begum. Being Babba Huzoor's oldest offspring, Mariam Begum, and her children after her, continued to live in the bada mahal. Kulsoom Begum married Mirza Firoz Bakht, a descendant of the Moghals, and moved to his haveli on Shivala Ghat. They had five children—three daughters and two sons, out of whom only a daughter, Akhtari Begum, was still around by the time I grew up. There was quite a bit of intermarrying between the relatives, which created many sets of double relationships. There were also no fewer judicial suits between them. Anwarul Hasan, whose hobby it was to file cases, could be spotted every day at the kutchery, taciturn, dressed in winter in a black shervani with the bottoms of his pyjamas tucked into his socks to prevent them from getting caught in the chain of the bicycle that was his primary mode of transport. Unmindful of the drain on the meagre resources from his zamindari rental, he sued his sister Nazneen Begum so many times for plotting to murder him that the judge, by then fed up, adjourned the case till the date when the sister had succeeded in murdering the brother.

Nazneen Begum's daughter Alia had been married to Haidar Ali Tabatabai of Lucknow, who conducted defensive legal proceedings against Anwarul Hasan in the 'murder' case. Alia Begum and her husband would visit Nawab-ki-Deorhi from Orderly Bazaar where they lived, bearing with them a basket from which emerged sheermals and paapas, flaky and puffed up with the air trapped in their many layers. The couple eventually moved to Nawab-ki-Deorhi and settled in the zard kamra, the 'yellow' room with walls completely white, the last in the row of four rooms adjacent to the front veranda. Haidar Ali predeceased his wife, and Alia Begum would be seen sitting on the takht in her room, her filarial swollen leg stretched out in front of her, looking dully at the octagonal clock that broke into a wheezing chime every hour, as though she were waiting for it to be time for her, too, to go. Each time I visited her in her room, she would, like an old tree shedding its last leaves, give me the things that she owned—a cut glass tray that had broken and been stitched back with the metal stitches showing, a small wooden casket of fine craftsmanship, a glass container with olive green and white stripes that held a vial of itra, and eventually the clock, as well as a raw silk screen mounted on a wooden frame with curving legs used as a room divider, and three tables, one with a marble top, that looked like they belonged to the last century.

By the 1960s, most of the older generation was dead, but Akhtari Begum, Kulsoom Begum's daughter, after marrying her cousin Anwarul Hasan, had moved to the bada mahal where she lived out her days. She was a pious old lady, and we'd find her sitting on a takht, the sheet held in place at the four corners by a mir farsh, which was an onion-shaped weight, about six inches high and with a four-inch wide square base, made of marble. She kept with her various holy items on the takht, including prayer books, a janamaz or prayer mat made of cloth and her tasbeeh, the rosary with ninety-nine radium beads that glowed in the dark and which she read several times a day. She also kept in a specially designed pocket in the prayer mat a sijdiga. This was a small round tablet of clay, worn smooth with use, on which she'd rest her head when she bowed during namaz. The clay tablet stood in for the soil from the battlefield in Karbala on which

Imam Hussain had been slain along with the rest of his family. There was a bottle of transparent green glass that held aab-e-zamzam, which I discovered was holy water from the Zamzam Well situated in a mosque in Mecca and not water from the Euphrates as I'd grown up thinking because the name Nahr al Furat kept cropping up in majlis readings. A few sips of it could ward off all kinds of disasters ranging from minor illnesses to more serious strokes of misfortune, and it was because of this, Akhtari Begum believed, that she was still alive when all the relatives her age had long bitten the dust. The aab-e-zamzam disappointingly tasted just the same as water.

Akhtari Begum had gone on a Hajj pilgrimage in the 1920s, travelling by ship from Bombay to Jeddah, a voyage that took a week and was probably the only time in her long life that she travelled. What the devout lady remembered from it half a century later was how her breasts had been admired, and she never tired of mentioning it, her voice dropping to a low confiding whisper. That her breasts had been sighted there, in the holiest of holy places where the rules demanded that all the parts of a woman's body be fully covered, was puzzling to say the least. She'd talk about her frugal meals, always saying that she 'used' rather than ate only two rotis. The other story from the Hajj pilgrimage was repeated by her so often that it had entered household legend. This was about the fish that she had caught on the ship. It was a rudimentary sort of ship in which the toilet chute opened right into the sea. While at her toilet one morning, she had felt a fish brush against her posterior. Not one to lose time, she had, in a trice, let a basket down through the aperture and caught the fish. But when she tried to pull the basket up, the fish was too heavy. She called out to her man-servant Soopan to come and help her. The man, a little aghast at first at being called by his mistress into the privy, finally picked up the courage to enter and helped her pull up the basket. It was an enormous fish, and all the passengers on the ship had a feast.

Akhtari Begum's son Ziaul Hasan, like his father Anwarul Hasan, would tuck the ends of his pyjamas into his socks when he rode a bicycle, and did one better than his father by wearing a bowler hat as well. He'd come over, unannounced, often at lunchtime, bringing a small offering of meat or dal, and would join us at our meal. A handsome man, he'd been forced by his father to study science though he had a leaning towards literature, and because of this early thwarting, he wore an air of reproach like a light overcoat, even as he read out long passages from P.G. Wodehouse whose books he loved. His congealed ambitions did not stray further than looking time and again at the family jewels locked away in the safe, and he'd talk of how his eyes were dazzled each time he saw them. And also about how he felt hammer-like blows descending on his chest each time he passed the house that he had once owned, but, with no income to speak of, had been forced to sell. A sense of drama, inherited from his mother, flowed through his veins like blood.

Two or three generations of Babba Huzoor's descendants had grown up in the haveli. Their eccentricities made up the fabric of some of the stories that my grandmother told us. One of them was about Shaheed Mard, the martyred man, who was known to skulk about in the dark. He was a wandering saint from who knew when and had taken a fancy to the house. Halima said he'd been climbing down the dusty stairs inside the waiting hall for the past hundred years and was still not done with them; he was always on his way down and had yet to reach the ground. If you climbed up to the roof, you could see his shrine, with his grave visible from outside; it was covered with green satin that had silver threadwork on it. Well, at least he was dead, as were all of our own forebears. My grandmother and my unmarried aunt, who was more like a second mother to us, were left in the house now, along with a few old retainers like Halima, Panna, and Sudarshan the gardener, all of whom had been living for a long time in the row of dark, wet rooms adjacent to the side entry door.

Thousands of sparrows had made their home in the ancient madhumalti creeper that ran all along the walls of the courtyard and started a raucous chirruping at daybreak, a cacophony loud enough to infiltrate the deepest sleep. My aunt shook the vine and they flew into the sky with a tremendous whirring of wings that seemed to set the entire space in motion. It was these chirruping sparrows that my maternal uncle, Mirza Mohammad Taqi, the one brother among three sisters, never forgot when he was in Beirut, where he lived for a few years on a UN posting. Recently I came upon perhaps the only story or at least the one still extant, that he wrote. It was set in the disintegrating Nawab-ki-Deorhi and appropriately titled 'Deemak' (Termites). It was published in the 1957 New Year issue of *Kahani*, the journal that my father edited. He kept thinking of compiling a dictionary of the Begamati Zabaan, the particular register of Urdu spoken by the women of the haveli, but he never got round to it. A decade later, he was dead, and buried in Beirut, far away from his beloved Nawab-ki-Deorhi. Since he was the sole male heir, with his migration to Pakistan, the house was appropriated by the custodian of properties, and it took much effort on my grandmother's part to retrieve the place.

Whenever I visited Nawab-ki-Deorhi, the stones of the house spoke to me. I could not understand what it was about the place that made my senses so keenly receptive, so much so that I seemed to hear ticking away the three clocks of unknown vintage on the mantelpiece in the drawing room—clocks that had been silent for years, and in their muteness, acquired the fixity of character to be met with in certain obstinate individuals. Yet I could hear them frenetically ticking, as if anxious to get the better of time. I kept returning to the haveli in my fiction, impelled by something larger than physical geography. Odours hung about the house, smells complexly composed of dust and the mustiness of rooms that had not been inhabited for years, of mice and of stagnant water from uncovered drains, of the steaming tea that my grandmother poured into the saucer before slurping it, of the subtle alchemy of khus from her burqa and the bidis that she smoked, of the charcoal aroma of kebabs on skewers being roasted on an open fire, of the viscous jalebis with their complicated curlicues bought from the nearby halwai, of pigeon shit and sparrow feathers. Or, it could simply have been the reek of old age that at night was overtaken by the heavy scent of madhumalti flowers and of jasmine. The sun came up early from behind Izhar's crumbling house and the wind scattered seeds along the parapets of the roofs so that when you looked up, you could see between yourself and the sky, dry grass and young banyans that were slyly extending their roots into the building. And from a milad somewhere close by, faint like a memory, on the dawn air would come the refrain of *ya nabi salam alaika, ya rasul salam alaika, ya habib salam alaika....*

When I returned to the place after my grandmother and my aunt were both dead, the old building was being pulled down to make way for a modern one. The house that had always seemed to be on the brink of extinction was finally embracing its fate. Half the building was already gone, and in its place was a vacant space with tall heaps of rubble along the sides. A few months later, the whole structure had been demolished, with no trace left of what it had earlier been, but for the stubborn madhumalti that kept pushing up out of the soil, even after being cut several times, in the place where it had always grown. I stood there, looking at the sky which was a vivid blue, and in it, birds, intensely black, and looking like the airborne cinders from a conflagration.

It was gone but I could still feel the house, rather like an amputee who has an enduring itch in their toe long after the leg has been removed. I could see my aunt going round the house in a state of agitation, searching for something. The key to the godaam had been misplaced. The godaam was a dark storeroom adjacent to the kitchen in which the rations were kept. It was home to generations of mice, and when you entered, you often got a glimpse, momentary like a whim, of shiny eyes and twitching tails as they disappeared behind the cupboard or the black trunk kept to one side. Rice, flour, sugar, grams and various kinds of lentils were stored there in brass containers that had a convex bottom, which caused them to wobble each time the lid was lifted. Then there was the mystery of the kitchen objects which it housed. They were things that had fallen into disuse, and no one now remembered what some of them had been used for. What use could that arrangement of thin beaten brass rings that were fused together possibly have had? Was it a stand, a case, a lid, an item of decoration? Its purpose had been lost and it was now simply a useless, if slightly mysterious, object. Other objects, if not mysterious, were still useless. The tall glass jar had a rusty lid fitted with a handle that, on being rotated, churned the jar's contents; in it, perhaps, curd had been made into butter. However, it had been a long time since butter was made in the house.

Remember! I said to myself. Remember all of those things. There were two sarautas in the godaam, the betel-nut cutters with ornate handles, one inlaid with bone. The blades had become blunt, but they seemed to have upon them the imprint of generations of women who had used them. Remember the Wedgwood dinner plates, the ones with the double bottom—the hollow space between the two bottoms had an opening closed with a cork, to release, after the meal, the hot water that kept the food warm. The plates must have broken or been gifted away. Remember ... remember ... remember.... There was a decanter with a round cut-glass lid, which in the brief sunshine that entered the room caught the evanescent quality of light. Remember the large embossed spittoon that looked too grand for its original purpose, remember the round paan-dan that had a faded pink silk cover, the glass itra-dans, which if you sniffed inside, still held within their yellowing interiors, the fading essence of scents long vanished. Remember too, the silver flower tray on the shelf, pock-marked with mildew stains and placed somewhat incongruously next to a lethal-looking chopper with a curved handle that brought to mind scenes of bloodshed. Remember each one of these things, for you will not set eyes on them again. My left thumb has broken into a jig. I cannot control it or stop the jigging. The self-willed thumb dances out its caprice and stops on its own. It is now still.

There were quite a few keys—to rooms, or cupboards, or trunks, and one of them would quite suddenly go missing; sometimes even whole bunches of keys would disappear.

'*Shaitan ki taang bandho*,' I hear my grandmother say.

It is the devil who causes things to get lost, and if you tie his leg the mislaid object is quickly found. Tying the devil's leg simply means tying a knot on a handkerchief or a scarf and, whether it is the spell working or just coincidence, whatever you are looking for is soon lighted upon.

Mother-in-law's tongue. *Dracaena trifasciata*. It sits before me in its clay pot, and I look at its pointed leaves that are like daggers.

The room, with the steady whirring of the fan, seems to be sailing away, propelled by the flapping curtains. My grandmother comes to me with her snowy hair and eagle eyes. The years must have wrought changes upon her, as she progressed from sunrise to sunset for almost a century, moulding her as nature modifies a landscape. There she is, absently mashing together roti and dal to feed her hens. *Aa aa aah!* She calls out to them. *Aa aa aah!* And the eight hens come running, all feathers, beaks and feet, pecking at the mess on the ground. She leans back and takes a long puff on her bidi. It's not bidi smoke but a calm that descends on her like a cloak. What does she think of at these times when she sits so quietly? Does she ever think of him, her long dead husband of forty-two years? She did not speak a word to him in the last twenty years of his life, up until his death in 1948. She'd found out that he had another woman. He is dead to her decades before he dies. Has a scab finally formed over her rage?

'*Shaitan ki taang bandho!*' echoes her voice. I tie a knot on the scarf I am wearing, a purple one—and details of the home I had spent so much time in, the people I had known there, the furniture and the objects in it, along with the smells and the sounds from half a century ago, emerge from beneath the detritus of the present. I'm looking for stasis, for a harmonious fixity. I want those people and the rooms they lived in to be fossilised, frozen—it is the past after all, and nothing more can happen in it. It's over. So, should it not, that rock hacked away from the cliff of time, be available to be written about? But looking into the past, what I find are quick shoals of fish, darting, surging, exploding, illusory, and but a play of light.

'They're all liars,' says my grandmother. 'Never believe what you hear.'

Blue Envelopes

It was the death of the monkey that haunted them.

She was a young female that had been brought to the Nawab-ki-Deorhi house in Banaras to perform the role of *jaape ka bandar*, which quite literally meant 'the labour monkey'. It was in the 1920s and, according to my mother, it was the prevalent belief in her family that if there was a monkey in the labour room when a child was born, the evil spirits that lay in wait for the newborn would cotton on to the monkey instead. Tough luck for the monkey, but that's what monkeys were there for. My grandmother was due to deliver a child, her last as it later turned out, a boy who did not survive infancy despite the monkey. It must have been a bit of a job finding the monkey. Were they sold in the market? At any rate, a male monkey had been hard to come by and they had settled for a young female. Everyone, but for an uncle, whose emotions—compassion, for example—were rather well hidden, grew fond of her. She wasn't got rid of after the birth as was usually done and became a pet. My grandmother stitched skirts for her, dressed her in bead necklaces and put a cap with silver trim on her head. She was incredibly delicate. She'd sit on my grandmother's shoulder and, her round eyes intent on their purpose, try to search with her thin fingers for lice in my grandmother's hair. My mother and my aunts went to the extent of getting lice put in their hair so the monkey would sit on their shoulders too and pick them out. This was all very well.

But then she did the unforgivable. She—in keeping with her monkey ways—broke the tender shoot that had appeared on the husn-e-hina, the henna bush in the courtyard. It was just her luck that this was the very bush that was being guarded jealously by the girls' uncle who couldn't stand her. Perhaps he used the leaves to dye his beard or his hair. And to compound the crime, the monkey ran away with his socks and chucked them on the roof. Of course, the socks were found later, but my mother's uncle certainly wasn't going to put up with any further antics of this spoilt monkey. From then on, he was after her blood. He got her one day, calling out to the servant to see where the monkey had fallen as he put away his gun. They never got over it, my mother, then eight years old, and her sister, who was three years older. My mother remembered the incident years later when she started writing stories and the monkey found her way into one of them titled 'Bandariya Badshahzadi' (The Monkey Princess). In it she related the events of the day when the monkey was killed. Of course, she had no inkling of the story at the time. The sisters were still learning Urdu and Farsi, which Maulvi Sahib had been engaged to teach them.

It was a bit of luck that Maulvi Sahib was an opium addict. He'd arrive every morning with a depressing inevitability. His coming was announced by the sound of his stick tapping as he made his way up the pebble-strewn gali that led to the house. And then, his distinctive cough would be heard at the door. It was a narrow door that opened directly onto the stone-flagged front veranda, a part of which was shaded by a jasmine creeper. The girls would hear the heavy iron chain on the door being jangled; this meant that they could no longer pretend they hadn't heard him coming. A servant would be sent to open the door, and there he'd be, thin as a stick, dressed in a black shervani buttoned up to the neck and a woollen cap on his head, with a book tucked under an arm and his stick held in the other hand, looking as if he'd been blown there by the wind. He'd sit and wait on the straight-backed chair that had been set out for him beside the takht on which was spread a very white sheet, each of its four corners held down by a marble mir farsh. The girls took their time coming. When they finally arrived, he would set them a lesson to memorise and, with eyes glazed under the effect of opium, watched them swaying back and forth to the rhythm of the words that they repeated. Soon he would be fast asleep and snoring gently.

My mother Zahra Begum and her sister Shamsunnahar Begum—called Moghal at home (for she was strong, as Moghals were thought to be)—were being homeschooled. They did not go to a formal school because they were supposed to be in purdah. Their older sister Ruqaiya, at the age of seven, had found to her dismay that she was suddenly forbidden to run and greet when he came, her favourite chacha, who was her father's friend, no blood relation, but considered an uncle nonetheless, and whom she adored. She was now in purdah, and the uncle had overnight become an 'outsider', for he was not a family member. Maulvi Sahib was an outsider too, but then he'd long been the family tutor and had also taught Ruqaiya Begum, the oldest and smartest of them all, who had a terrific memory and could reel off long poems after having read them only a couple of times. She had been married at the age of fourteen to a much older man, who, by a complicated thread of kinship, was also her uncle, and had left home. And Maulvi Sahib had also taught the one brother among the three sisters, Taqi Miyan.

After Maulvi Sahib had been sleeping for a while, one of the girls picked up a large stone and struck it against an old tin tray that they got from the kitchen, to mimic the crashing noise made by the Town Hall gong that sounded at noon. The gong signalled the end of the lesson. Maulvi Sahib woke with a start, thought that he'd been there for a whole hour and shuffled off after having set them work for the next day. What with these pranks, the sisters couldn't have learnt much, you would have thought. Yet they became well-versed in the works of the major Urdu and Farsi poets, Mir, Ghalib and Zauq, Saadi and Hafiz, among others. They were always ready with an apt couplet for every occasion and were constantly taking apart and putting together again, as though dealing with complicated machinery, lines from couplets, discussing rhyme and metre and how the balance of a couplet could be ruined by the use of an unnecessary word. They didn't write poetry, but poetry was woven into the fabric of their lives. Sometimes, just for the heck of it, they'd fashion their own couplets out of the lines written by a famous poet. It was the early lessons with Maulvi Sahib that must have come in handy when, much later, they started writing in Urdu the stories that they subsequently transcribed into Nagari for ease of publication and for a wider readership. Many of them were published in the 1960s in *Kahani*, the journal that my father edited, or in *Kalpana*, *Dharmayug*, *Nai Kahaniyan* and a few other magazines of the time.

For the stories, they drew on the material that was available to them in the world of the haveli in which they grew up, and even though both the sisters wrote about the same world, their stories each had an individual, distinctive character. The language itself, the everyday Urdu that they used in conversation was dying out, along with the world of the haveli. Fading begums peopled that world, as did spendthrift nawabs and their retainers, the coachman, the cook, the gardener and the stable-boy. Sometimes there'd be a midwife, or the ghassalni, the woman whose job it was to bathe dead bodies. It was an insular world with its gaze turned inward, claustrophobic and clinging to notions of grandeur and class hierarchy, to centuries' old traditions that had no link to the changed world outside. There was an underlay of irony in the sisters' depiction of this world in which the melancholy of failed lives bred resentments and cruelty. In the act of being written, the stories simultaneously became a record of the haveli, and a critical assessment. Written with a detachment reminiscent of Chekhov, free of judgement or censure, the stories were embedded in their context. And yet it was the dispassionate voice in which they were written that took the characters out of the haveli and placed them on a larger human canvas. The titles of the stories were suggestive—'Maurusi Jaydad' (The Inheritance), 'Vasiyatnama' (The Will), 'Tumhein to Maut hi Ati Shabab ke Badle' (Death Should Have Come to You, Not Youth], 'Vida' (The Farewell), 'Mahalsara ka Ek Khel' (A Game in the Women's Quarter), and it was under this last title that their work was subsequently collected decades after their creators had died.

During the years that Maulvi Sahib taught them, the sisters knew no Nagari, nor for that matter English. They were encouraged to learn both of these languages by Taqi Miyan who was a few years older than them and already going to college. It was because of him that two Englishwomen, Miss Nicholson and Miss Johnson, were engaged by turns as English teachers for his sisters. The teachers brought books for them to read—*Jessica's First Prayer* by Hesba Stretton and *Saved at Sea* by Mrs O.F. Walton, both published by the Religious Tract Society in 1867 and 1887, respectively, and both were Christian stories. *Saved at Sea* described a terrible storm. There was a lighthouse on the rocks, and by its revolving beam of light, a ship that looked to be in trouble was spotted. Someone threw down a bundle from the sinking ship and it was caught by the man from the lighthouse. The bundle contained a blue-eyed child called Timpey, who was given shelter and cared for by the lighthouse man and his grandson. She was a 'sunbeam' and she brought into their lives a stirring of better, heavenly things. The story was a quick little allegory about salvation and the perfect plan of God's love, asking the two central characters (and the readers) to look inwards and see if their 'foundation' was built on rock or on sand. The message from the Bible that the book held out was contained in two short lines from Matt. VII. 25, which the sisters with their long practice at memorising learnt at once:

On Christ, the solid rock I stand,
All other ground is sinking sand.

Their mother, a staunch Shia, might have had a thing or two to say about her daughters' brush with Christianity, but she had no idea of the books the girls were reading. Her response to the two English teachers was her usual amused aloofness, and her one comment on Miss Nicholson, who was the first of the two teachers, was that she looked insipid, like a turnip without salt.

Apart from these two books of Christian fiction, I found a third in our house that had my mother's name inscribed on the fly-leaf. It was *Health and Beauty by a Beauty Expert* from the *Pearson's Modern Handbooks* series. All three books had been partly destroyed by wood borers and were marked with holes that looked like tiny bullet marks. I realised as soon as I opened the book by the beauty expert that it could not have been brought into the house by the two English ladies. It must have been acquired later by my mother, probably on the eve of her marriage to my father, and she had brought it along with her from the Nawab-ki-Deorhi house when she got married. The book had chapters on how to make each part of the woman's body beautiful. The chapter headings—'Eyes Right!', 'Sound Teeth', 'Beautiful Hands', 'Lovely Limbs', 'Foot Faults', 'The Daily Dozen'—made you curious to know more about how the perfection was to be achieved. But the two most exciting chapters were the ones called 'Reducing Baths' and 'Various Reducing Gadgets'. 'Reducing Baths' listed a whole range of baths for getting rid of excess weight, including Soda and Borax Baths, Epsom Salt Baths, Turkish Baths and Foam Baths. For the last of these, you could buy at the chemist's, a packet of Dr. Ecklund's Foam Bath Crystals that in England cost two shillings and six pennies; a wire whisk for beating up the foam was included in the deal. The baths required you to immerse yourself up to the chin and stay soaked for a considerable duration in the rather hot water that was saturated with salts. From the soaking, you emerged lighter and with a 'sylph-like' figure. If it was not the whole body that needed reducing but only a particular part, there was a bath for that too. In addition to these, there was a list of ingredients for a Home-made Reducing Bath and a Special Reducing Fluid. There were rather intriguing 'reducing' gadgets too—the Massage Roller, the Vibratone, the Lecco Stimulator, the Punch Ball, and at the end of it all, the modest skipping rope.

My mother was supposed to look like Nargis. It was one of the sayings that my father had carelessly flung into the air in the days of their courtship. He wasn't keen on Hindi cinema and, in fact, in later years, he prevented us from seeing Hindi films or listening to film music, for he thought that it would corrupt our taste. And yet he had chosen to compare his beloved to a film star. There was a photograph from her youth in the tin box spotted with rust that had no lid and which was stuffed with old photos, with their yellow paper curling at the edges. The box had once contained rolls of film for my father's Agfa camera. My mother was lying on a cheetah skin that had the cheetah's head intact, and the antlers of a stag were up on the wall behind her. The cheetah's wide open eyes were glazed, the mouth open in a snarl with the fang-like teeth showing—it had been killed in the act of defending itself. Its face made a contrast with my mother's, right above it. Her expression was thoughtful, with the hint of a smile on her lips. She was wearing a sari and a frilly blouse with short sleeves that showed her rounded arms. She said she'd been sixteen when the photo was taken, but she looked older in it. Her face was still pretty much the same when she was in her sixties. She never forgot my father's teasing compliment comparing her with Nargis, and her face would light up each time someone mentioned it.

They must have been in love. My father was her brother Taqi Miyan's friend from university and he came rather frequently to the house to meet him. Or so everyone thought. But he flirted with both the sisters. And soon the dalliance took on a more serious air. Was he trying to make up his mind to marry, and if so, which of the two sisters was he interested in? My mother, in her story 'Aam ke Baur' (Mango Blossoms) wrote about that time, about her brother's friends who dropped by, presumably to meet him, the card games, the banter and the confusions of first love that reached their culmination in a kiss. It was a bold story for the times, skilfully intertwining the triple threads of physical love, a love for music, and an immersion in nature. Her letters to him, both before and after they got married, were flirtatious and despondent by turns. The early letters, facetious in tone, spoke of a Miss Hardy and a Miss Tripathi, of the 'English beauties' and also of 'the one from the Savoy Hotel', referring to them as the 'new catastrophe' that had descended upon him (she always addressed him as 'S' in the letters) just when he had somehow managed to survive what she called the unwelcome attentions of the earlier set of women, each prettier than the other. She called him a 'poor little mite' who was forced to entertain so many young women, all crazy about him, and then immediately switched to a plaintive tone, bemoaning how she missed him even as she counted the many days till they could meet again. She wrote two or three letters to him daily and, sweating it out in the intense heat of the Allahabad and Banaras summers, he'd be on the lookout for the post that brought the blue envelopes that held her letters. In the early years of their marriage, she spent the summers in the Kumaon hills, while he stayed behind in the plains to sort out the publishing business that had yet to bring in enough money for them to live comfortably. Most of the letters that he wrote, transversely across the page in his distinctive hand, were sent to Pushkar Cottage, Nainital or to Rockwood, Mussoorie, and there were a couple that were later sent to Oakley, Ranikhet.

It had not been easy for them when they wanted to get married in 1948. Neither of them was religious, but it was soon after Partition, and Hindu–Muslim antagonism was particularly high. The air was thick with news of killings, of trains leaving or arriving from Lahore or Amritsar stuffed with corpses, and yet, in my mother's letter written on 10 October 1947, less than two months after Partition, there was no mention of the violence even as she spoke about going to the station to see my father off, expressing her distress at having to do this so often. My father who was Premchand's elder son, a liberal Hindu, and my mother with her Shia Muslim background were hardly an ideal match given the times. My maternal grandmother threatened to jump into a well. My father's mother, who was herself of small physique, jibed about how after years of waiting, the 'lamboda' or the 'long' daughter-in-law was here at last. No one from my mother's family, except for her eighteen-year-old nephew, Ruqaiya Begum's son, came to the wedding, which was conducted under civil law and was followed by a modest celebration held at 14 Hastings Road in Allahabad, where my father was living at the time with a group of writer friends. However, all the acrimony disappeared with the birth of my brother, their first-born.

In a letter to my father written from Rockwood, Mussoorie in July 1954, almost six years after they got married, my mother told him that she had run out of paper, presumably because of the many letters she wrote to him, and that she hadn't written to him on 'good' paper for a long time. She realised, she said, that her blue envelopes did not have the same effect on his heart now as they earlier did, but she had still thought to buy a new letter pad to write to him. That their relationship had by now settled into the stasis of marriage was evident. But perhaps part of the reason for the blue envelopes having lost their impact lay elsewhere. In one of his letters written in 1954, to which my mother's letter about the blue envelopes may have been a reply, my father hinted at having conflicted feelings, going on to say that his thoughts now and then returned to the time when he had been close to both the sisters. It was a subject that had cropped up between them earlier too. My mother reminded him of how years ago, at the start of their romance, she'd half jokingly suggested he take her beloved sister as his shareek-e-hayat or life partner instead of her, and at that point he had said to her, 'If you're trying to shake me off it's another matter, but this hunter knows his quarry.' But now he seemed again to swing, pendulum-like, between the two of them. Having written about the struggle with his feelings, he returned, in another letter written the same year, to the sentiment that he'd earlier expressed:

> You think that having made you my wife I am forgetting you, or have already forgotten you. But this is wrong. In my eyes,

> you are still my beloved of six years ago, though now I may find it awkward to keep expressing it unnecessarily. I care deeply for Moghal, I have never kept this a secret from you, nor will I do so in the future. But this has nothing to do with my love for you. They are two different kinds of feelings.

My aunt did not write a story about those days when my father would visit the Nawab-ki-Deorhi house, and whatever letters she may have written have not survived, except for one. It is written in an almost illegible hand in Urdu to my father, and the date on the postmark is 28 March 1948, seven months before he married my mother. The tone of the letter is one of hurt but dignified acceptance of the situation. In later years, she had about her a faint aura of sadness, though she was so full of witty remarks and wisecracks that you could hardly have said she was sorrowful. In the letter, she called my father 'Bhai', a form of address for men that was, at the time, considered appropriate for use by unmarried women. She went on to talk about how much he had changed, how she had been foolishly unaware of the transformation, which was now so obvious that even a blind person could see it. The letter seemed to suggest that beneath the overtly stated and rather flamboyant love that my father had for my mother, there had perhaps been a hidden seam of love for her as well.

There is no doubt that the ties between the three of them were complex. It could have been that the sibling bonding between the two sisters was stronger than any romantic entanglements that they had, and it was this bond that endured, eventually unscathed, till the end of their lives. In the early nineties, when my aunt had already had the first of the heart attacks that would eventually claim her life, sensing perhaps that the end was near, she expressed the feeling she often had, that her life had gone by and she hadn't even noticed. It was then that she'd also told her sister that perhaps now it was time for her to go. 'Nonsense!' my mother said. 'We're both going together and I don't intend to go any time soon.' It was as if a pact was sealed between them just then. My mother's statement turned out to be prophetic. The sisters did indeed die on the same night.

For my siblings and for me, they functioned as interchangeable mothers, and it seemed entirely natural that our mother with her innate and congenital fertility should have given birth to us, and our aunt who visited often from Banaras and seemed to be the more motherly of the two, should have such a large part in nurturing us. My father did 'care deeply' for my aunt too, though in later years this might have been difficult to guess. He could have been in a spectacularly foul mood on the day when she asked him for one of his paintings—the canvases which he had no hesitation in gifting even to complete strangers. Maybe he remembered a fraught past with her and his 'conflicted' feelings just then. Whatever may have provoked it, his answer to her at that point was—'I don't like beggars'. And so it was that till the end of their lives not a single painting of his could be found on the walls of Nawab-ki-Deorhi, whereas the Drummond Road house at Allahabad seemed to be choked with them.

It was my aunt who compared him to Harry Haller in the Herman Hesse novel of 1927, *Steppenwolf*, a man who had two contradictory souls, the 'wolf of the steppes' that yearned for isolation but at the same time sought the comfort of society and of love. This was a convenient explanation for my father's unpredictable moods. But it was true that on certain evenings I could hear him arguing bitterly with my mother long after we'd gone to bed, and on others he was sweetness itself. After my aunt's death, while clearing the drawer of her old writing desk, I came upon her copy of *Steppenwolf*, and when I read it later, I could see why she had drawn that comparison. She was a woman of understated emotion, except for the one time in 1948, when having just heard the news of Mahatma Gandhi's assassination, she had burst out in agitation that if the killer was found to be a Muslim, she'd commit suicide.

The centuries old Nawab-ki-Deorhi house seemed to be falling to pieces. There was mould on the walls where water had seeped in, particularly after a heavy rainy season, there were weeds and banyan saplings growing on the roof and reaching into the brickwork, the wooden beams were being eaten away by termites, and repairs were constantly needed. Her mother was old, her brother had left the country at the time of Partition, and her two sisters were both caught up in their domestic lives in Allahabad. There was no one she could have asked to share the expenses for the maintenance of the house even if she had been inclined to do so. But there was her pride to reckon with. In 1966, she established, with a sense of purpose and liberal ideals, a school for children within the precincts of the house. Some of the proceeds from this school could now be used for the upkeep of the house. She continued to run the school till the end of her life, working at her desk even till a few hours before her death. Shaping the lives of a whole generation of children brought meaning to her life as well, and she became the motivating force behind her sisters setting up branches of the same school in Allahabad.

If my father's feelings for my aunt had been ambiguous, it was not that he approved either, of my mother's quick bursts of energy, of her almost primal creative instincts. It was as if she could not bear the idea of colourlessness. She reworked the faded embroidery on an old Kashmiri tea cosy to enhance it beyond its original brightness, used leftover wool to knit sweaters in patchwork patterns of her own invention, the clay pots on which she painted flowers were one of the sources of inspiration for my father when he started painting—things that she put her hand to seemed to come awake and stretch themselves. Most of the cuttings of bougainvillea, of rose, or jasmine that she stuck into the ground took root. In the patch of land at the far back of the garden, she'd set up a rose nursery called The Garden of Roses. She propagated new plants there and sold them for Rs 2 each. It was hardly a business, but it certainly gave her something to do. A thin booklet with a light pink cover listed the names of the roses—*Garden Party, Iceberg, Eiffel Tower, Peace, Black Prince, Independence, Montezuma,* the multi-coloured *Joseph's Coat*; she'd spend hours writing out their names on strips of tinfoil and attaching them to the plants. The roses were pruned on 15 October each year, and the cut flowers were placed everywhere in buckets filled with water. They added colour to the dark interiors of the house, and their rather heavy, carnal scent would spread through the rooms as long as the blooms lasted. The years had slowly been changing her loving husband of the early years of their marriage who wrote eager letters to her and waited for her blue envelopes. He had become a taciturn man of few words who 'hated being moved about'. She was baffled by the elusiveness of his personality, the dark and changeable edge of him that was quite inaccessible to her. Her fecundity in turn caused him to feel a sort of aesthetic distaste; the bubbling up of her desires and her constant impulse to life that she seemed unable to curb appeared unseemly to him and led him to comment that she was greedy for things.

If he had moved away from her, so had she from him, coming ever closer to her sister. Both of them loved drinking tea. We'd wake on winter mornings, while it was still dark and the doors were still closed to keep out the cold, to the clinking sound of the tea things being arranged on a tray. We'd hear them talking in low voices as the day brightened outside the window. They seemed always to be drinking tea, pouring out the amber infusion from the round China teapot that seemed to hold in its belly an endless quantity of Lopchu's Flowery Orange Pekoe. As the house came awake, the family gathered round the teapot. At these times, sitting together, I felt we were conspirators, drawn into a close circle which somehow also included the rakish card players in Paul Cezanne's painting, a reproduction of which hung on the wall right above us.

My aunt was used to her cigarettes as well, and her preferred brand was Four Square. The cigarettes came in a small white packet that had, as if for emphasis, four green squares printed on it. When we visited Nawab-ki-Deorhi, my mother too would join her in the sehenchi. They'd sit together and smoke on the sofa with the back-rest of woven cane, tipping the ash carelessly on the stone floor and never seeming to run out of things to say. There was a time when my mother had been a regular smoker too, but she'd had to give it up because of her singing, for the cigarettes affected her throat.

The sisters had discovered singing when they were still kids. It could have begun with the nauhas, the soz, and the marsiysas during Muharram. The elegiac poems had complicated classical tunes that were sonorously rendered by their mother. They had grown up listening to her voice. They found an empty copper pot in the courtyard and sang into it, discovering that the pot had the quality of amplifying sound. My mother said that it occurred to her then, with some surprise, that the sound coming from the pot was her own voice, and that it was an instrument that could be used for singing. Singing became a lifelong passion with her, but my aunt realised that it was not for her, though she continued to be an eager listener. My mother never became a professional singer, though she took lessons from some of the best practitioners of Hindustani classical music, including Ustad

Faiyaz Khan, who in 1908 had been given the title of *Aftab-e-Mousiqui*—the sun of music—by the Maharaja of Mysore.

In 1944, they invited him to perform at the local Hindustani music circle that my mother and some of her contemporaries had started in Banaras. He had been put up at Nawab-ki-Deorhi. He'd sit in the kitchen shelling peas with them, and all the while he gave my mother lessons. The ustad's performance at the music club was a striptease. He sang a passionate Jaijaiwanti, and feeling the heat as he warmed up to the singing, he first took off his turban, then his shervani that was decorated with all the medals with which he'd been honoured, then his inner waistcoat, till he was finally wearing only a thin muslin kurta. When they came back home later, he asked my mother to play on the HMV gramophone Raga Jaijaiwanti sung by various artistes, and listened to the renditions with an expression of disdain on his face. Then he said, 'Now put on my Jaijaiwanti.' He sat back with eyes closed in rapture and said, '*Wah!*'

My mother wrote to him after his visit, and he wrote back in an elaborate, courteous Urdu from Lakkadpitha, Baroda. The paper on which he wrote had his titles, along with his name, inscribed in quaint spelling on the letterhead: '*Gnan Ratna*' '*Aftab-e-Musiki*' '*Sangit Samrat*' *Ustad Phaiyaj Khan*. My mother preserved his letters. I found them, brittle and yellow with age, among her things after she died. There was also a photograph of him in which he was wearing a turban and had all his medals pinned on to his shervani. I counted nineteen of them. The photo stood, dog-eared and dusty, on the little wooden shelf above my mother's desk. And years later, the details preserved as though frozen under ice, my mother returned to the Jaijaiwanti performance in her story 'Aam ke Baur' (Mango Blossoms).

Reading: A Love Story

'Read!' said Santa Claus, and I began to read:

> *One day, a little girl called Alice lay under a tree in a wood. Her sister was reading a book, and Alice was dreaming …*

I was eight years old, in class four, at St Mary's Convent School in Allahabad, and Santa Claus taught us reading. The lesson was called 'Alice in Wonderland', from the *Radiant Way English Reader, Fourth Step*. The slim little book had on the cover two children tripping down a flower-strewn hillside, while two rabbits, their ears perked up, looked on.

Santa Claus was Sister Stanislaus, but everyone called her Santa Claus, though never to her face. For a long time, I did not find out her real name, and when I did, it was a tongue-twister. It just seemed easier to go on privately calling her Santa Claus. She looked nothing like the Santa on Christmas cards or in book illustrations. She was a wizened, slightly bent-over nun, who wore the white habit of the Roman Catholic order she belonged to, with her dark hair peeping out from beneath the wimple that was tight on her narrow forehead. She wore a silver crucifix which shone on her shrunken chest like a fallen star. When school got over, she'd stand under the tamarind tree near the gate with a long black folded umbrella in her hand, with which she'd tap on the head any child who happened to be out of line. She had come all the way from Kerala to become a nun. There was a bitter expression on her nut-brown face that looked like a purse made of old leather. In the thirty or so years she'd been at the school, she had waited in vain for the gratitude she felt the world owed her. Her shrewd bad-tempered little eyes took in the four rows of small fidgety girls sitting before her. We were a class of thirty-six.

'You!' she'd say, pointing randomly at any one of us. 'You! Next!' and the girl in question had to stand up and read the next paragraph while Santa Claus listened, tensed like a tigress, ready to spring at any hesitation or mistake in the reading. Sometimes she'd throw a piece of chalk at the girl she wanted to identify. It was difficult to predict who she would point to next, so everyone lived in equal dread. You had to sit up straight and were not allowed to whisper, lean across to each other, or look out of the window. There was a little garden outside the window, and in it a grotto, within which stood Virgin Mary in a flowing blue robe, calmly oblivious to the torments that Santa Claus regularly visited upon us. Beyond the garden, at the end of the drive was the green gate outside which the reign of the nuns ended.

'Sister, can I go out?' It was one of the new girls. She had dared to speak and that too, without raising her hand, or standing up. She was wholesomely squashed by Santa Claus.

'You *can*, but you *may not*.'

The little interlude had diverted her attention from me.

'Next!' she barked, and weak with relief, I sat down.

I'd read *Alice in Wonderland* at home, but reading aloud from this abridged version was something else. To begin with, it was quite different, but the setting and the story still bore enough resemblance to the original to be unsettling. Even in their watered-down form, the words reminded me of the ones I had so far read only to myself. And they now sounded strange, standing there on their own, unprotected as it were, without the shelter of my mind inside which they had until now lived. I didn't know how to say some of them. It was the first time that I had *heard* the words, and they had an alien feel, having somehow been robbed of their familiarity. What was more, Alice herself had turned traitor. I had secretly believed her to be only mine, but there she was, out in the open, lying under a tree and dreaming. I felt betrayed.

This was just the first betrayal. My possessiveness extended, over the years, to several characters in the books at our Drummond Road house, and it was always something of a shock to discover that others had known these books much before I had. I fell in love easily, and the list of my bookish infatuations was long. The girls at school had friends; I had books. I did not want anyone to even look at my books, let alone read them, and I guarded them jealously. For one, I had a horror of books with broken spines and dog ears, and I could not bear mine to be handled. There was a time when I was reluctant to read a new book myself, for fear of damaging the spine. I clung passionately to Catherine and Heathcliff in Emily Brontë's *Wuthering Heights*, a secret confidante of their frenzied love; to Pip in Dickens' *Great Expectations*, even though he was annoying; and I thought I knew Anna Karenina better than she knew herself. I never really took to Jane from Charlotte Brontë's *Jane Eyre*, whom I considered priggish, but that did not prevent me from climbing into the branches of a lime tree that was in full bloom, and there, hidden from view, I finished the book. Now and then, in stray Proustian moments, the scent of lime blossoms still brings back to me the atmosphere of the book, most of which seemed to have taken place in a dreary, wintry setting where lime blossoms could not possibly have blossomed. And this has been true for other books too. They have been conscientious 'memory keepers' and have marked off, as on a literary calendar, the times and the seasons in which I read them.

I grew up reading almost exclusively in English, and that too, primarily British literature. Looking back on it now, and especially as Hindi later became my chosen language for writing fiction, it was odd for books in Hindi or Urdu not to have figured on my childhood and teenage reading list. Surely one's mother tongue would be the first language one read in? Yet, if you had an English-medium education, you inevitably did most of your reading in English; there were books like *Lorna Doone, Little Women, What Katy Did, What Katy Did Next,* and *How Green Was My Valley* in the schoolroom cupboard that usually stayed locked, making even those books hard to get your hands on, except in the fortnightly library period. There was no literature available in other languages, and certainly none from the Indian languages. And how could there have been, when speaking Hindi even in the lunch break was frowned upon? Even so, the whole language issue was fraught with confusion. Like others of my background, I had a different 'speaking' first language, which was a mix of Hindi and Urdu, and a 'reading' first language, which was English. The Hindi period at school was only forty minutes out of the six hours we spent at school every day, and the lessons in the textbook were singularly dull and discouraging. They did not inspire you to read more Hindi books. We had Sanskrit till class six. You mugged up the lessons by heart to somehow pass the exam; they did not equip you to read any Sanskrit literature. The prune-faced maulvi who came to teach us Urdu at home was a thin, stern man called Talib Jaipuri. He lived in the quarters at the back of our house. He made you feel jittery in the hour spent with him, because at any sign of distraction or boredom, he could suddenly give you a painful rap on the knuckles with his pencil. I didn't learn how to read Urdu from his lessons, and had to wait till my mother decided to teach me and my siblings herself. She'd make us memorise Urdu poems, the cadences, the flow and the rhythm of Urdu slowly seeped into my linguistic consciousness, though it remained dormant for a long time.

The three languages that I knew with varying levels of fluency were permeated and coloured by the other languages that I heard around me. I grew up, like others in India, in the midst of what could perhaps be described as a palimpsest of languages. I arrived at reading fiction in Hindi, and then in Urdu, when I was in my twenties, and even then, it was all quite random, with no particular order to the books I read—I had no idea why I had picked them in the first place. Accustomed as I was to reading easily in English, for a while, Hindi texts needed some effort to get into. Urdu words often occurred in the Nagari script of a Hindi text, and these came with their own irritants. For the Urdu words, divorced from their nastaliq script, had to be written with nuqtas or diacritic marks below the letters for correct enunciation. Yet in Nagari, the nuqtas were often put in the wrong place, or not put at all, and this went against the linguistic grain of Urdu. The wrong placement of the diacritics set the teeth on edge, like screechy chalk on a school blackboard. Reading, I discovered, was a physical experience as well as a visual and mental one. That it was olfactory too, I had realised as a child, when I climbed up to the long room on top of the bungalow called Oakley in Ranikhet, which my father rented over several successive summers. The low-roofed room was full of old books with their musty smell. I remember from that collection a fascinating picture book about dogs.

In my early childhood, there had been the Enid Blyton books—they were the most easily available and regular fare then for children in provincial towns—and I ate my way through them, much as a caterpillar munches through a leaf, till I had run through the whole lot. Each Enid Blyton cost two rupees and sixty-five paisa, and I regularly amassed the sum from the loose change that I found lying about the house. Then, on a trip to Civil Lines, I'd disappear, usually with my sister who shared my enthusiasm, inside Universal Book Company, trying to hurriedly choose from the treasure trove on the shelves, while the family waited impatiently in the car. I emerged with the precious item, and it became imperative to write one's name on the fly-leaf as soon as we got home. It was as much about owning the books as about reading them.

My involvement with Enid Blyton reached a stage when I became her. I found myself scribbling words that she might have written. Two of the stories, among others ghost written by me at the age of eight, for Enid Blyton, were 'Lucky Horace' and 'Over the Hills and Far Away'. The latter was set in a cool, hilly place with bluebells and daffodils, a far cry from the hot plains of eastern Uttar Pradesh, where I lived. I soon outgrew Enid Blyton and the transition to Agatha Christie and then to Daphne du Maurier was smooth, if a little sudden. Both had a knack for writing a gripping tale, for building up atmosphere, and both, especially Christie, for creating brain teasers.

It was around this time that my mother had a small brick canal built in the garden to carry the water from one end of the orchard to another. It was connected to a large tank at the edge of the garden, and when you turned the faucet, the water would go gushing through the canal. We would sail paper boats in it. There was a row of old and tall sweet lime trees that would bend over it, creating a shady green tunnel. It was the perfect spot to sit undisturbed and read Harper Lee's *To Kill a Mockingbird* that was in our school curriculum and, among others, books by the Brontës, by George Eliot, by Jane Austen, or Daphne du

Maurier. Is it possible to have a memory of a place never visited? Sweet lime trees have somehow got mixed up for me with Cornwall, the setting of many of the du Maurier books, and this, I find, is where memory intersects with imagination. The tank at the edge of the garden, the canal built by my mother, and my mother herself, have all now vanished, but the shady green tunnel in my memory endlessly overlaps with the Cornwall of my teenage years, a place I never visited and am now unlikely to. An imagined place has become a remembered one.

Occasionally, one read *Tales from the Panchtantra*, the *Jataka Tales*, or *Aesop's Fables*, but they all ended with a moral. It felt like another betrayal. You were expecting a story, and you got a lesson. The *Arabian Nights*, of which there was an illustrated copy in the house, was rather more exciting, especially since my grandmother would, now and then, tell us the same stories from the Urdu version called *Alif Laila*. Ours was a non-religious household, even though my maternal grandmother, who often visited us from Banaras, was a practising Muslim. But neither of the grannies ever told us tales from the scriptures, from the *Ramayana* or the *Mahabharata*, from the *Puranas* or from the *Quran*. It was a singular deprivation that was never quite compensated, except in some ways, through reading. I was in love with reading.

Soon, the books in the drawing room cupboard stopped looking to me like furniture, and presented themselves as something to be read. Apart from my father's collection, there were also the ones that belonged to his friend Anand Krishna Pande. Ani Chacha, as we called him, had left Allahabad for a variety of reasons—one of them being the town's scheming mosquitoes that seemed to have a particular taste for his blood—and had stored his books at our place, to be dealt with later. It was a whole library. There were quite a few heavyweights among them. Lined up all together on the bookshelf, they formed a rather formidable phalanx. I settled on Sartre, and decided to read his trilogy, *The Roads to Freedom*. It consisted of *The Age of Reason, The Reprieve* and *Iron in the Soul*. I must have been out of my mind. I really don't know what attraction those tomes could, at fifteen, have had for me. Maybe I was going through a masochistic phase. Stoically, I waded through the Sartre marshland, getting bogged down on almost every page, reading with my eyes, not with my brain. Even when I finally made it to the end, I had no clue about what it was that I had just read. By the time I was an adult, my mind had created a sort of Sartre-block, and a subsequent effort to re-read the books still failed to yield meaning. It was like trying to wring water from a stone.

Proust was French too, but he was a different story altogether. I came to him much later, at the age of forty-one, even though he had all along been in the same cupboard that held the books by Sartre. And could one ever be the same after having heard that intimate, clairvoyant voice? The prose was elaborate, formal, analytical and poetic, composed of the famously long Proustian sentences, and possessed a psychological acuteness that seemed to see right into the soul. And he was funny. There were only two volumes left from my father's set of the 1945 Chatto & Windus edition of *Remembrance of Things Past*, translated by C.K. Scott Moncrieff. One of the two volumes was *Swann's Way: Part 1*, and I subsequently bought the Vintage edition of *In Search of Lost Time*, which was a revision by D.J. Enright of Terence Kilmartin's acclaimed revision of the original Moncrieff translation. It was published in 1996 and came in six volumes. It didn't take me long to figure out that here was a writer whose work one didn't merely read; one lived by it. Nabokov summed up the book thus:

> The transmutation of sensation into sentiment, the ebb and tide of memory, waves of emotions such as desire, jealousy, and artistic euphoria—this is the material of this enormous and yet singularly light and translucent work.

My discovery of Proust happened around the time I found myself living in East Delhi in an apartment block that was right across the road from where Nirmal Verma lived. I had known him for several years, having first met him when he came to Allahabad in the late eighties to deliver a lecture, and had kept up correspondence with him from Melbourne, where I lived till the early nineties, working at various jobs. We'd meet often at his place, and most of the conversation was about books and reading. He seemed to have read everything, apparently all the books that were there to be read. I once asked him how he had read so much. 'But that is all I've ever done,' he said. It was as if all the books he'd written had been written by someone else. I'd just finished reading *Swann's Way* and was in a state of confused euphoria, filled with a desire to talk about the book, and he seemed to be the obvious person to talk to. I've forgotten why we met at Ginza, in Connaught Place, but here was the perfect chance to ask him what he thought of the book. He looked at me for a long time with his large, serene, and dreamy eyes, and just when I thought he was about to speak, he said nothing. We sat there for about an hour and talked about grief, and love, and happiness, but he never directly answered my question about *Swann's Way*.

A few years ago, when I came upon the Swiss writer Robert Walser, I wondered whether Nirmalji had read him too and what he thought about him. It was too late to find out. Walser wrote short pieces, essays or stories, some no more than a page. I couldn't quite explain the effect he had on me. It was the slightly giddy quality of his prose—the excited voice that W.G. Sebald described as emanating from 'pure despair'—that took you to vertiginous heights and left you suspended there. But as soon as you shut the book, the sentences tended to vanish. Reading him was like reading yourself. It was a voice that spoke close to your ear, and yet was mysteriously elusive. It disappeared almost before you could hear it.

It was while translating the stories of Vinod Kumar Shukla into English that I found in them something of the vertiginous quality that I associated with Walser. It was an unlikely likeness. Shukla rarely left Raipur where he lived; he didn't read English and certainly hadn't read any European literature. In Shukla, the giddy quality resided in the formation of the sentences themselves, rather than in the voice. For instance, in 'Teen Billiyaan' (Three Cats), he wrote, 'Sometimes one saw at the same time three or four cats. To see three cats at the same time was like seeing three times the act of seeing the three cats.' The resemblance didn't end there. Both writers were obsessed with the ordinary. 'We don't need to see anything out of the ordinary, we already see so much,' Walser says in one of his stories. In Shukla, the ordinary could turn into something wondrous. For instance, an ordinary man walking down an ordinary street could be seen to have two noses. Or a roadways bus could begin to travel at great speed through the air.

I started reading the Russians in my teens, and continued to read them well into my thirties and forties. *War and Peace*, with its epic proportions, was obese and intimidating. But the Russian humourist Teffi, a younger contemporary of Tolstoy, had read it at the age of thirteen. I read her amusing account of reading *War and Peace* in her memoiristic piece, 'My First Tolstoy'. She was in love with Prince Andrei Bolkonsky and hated Natasha Rostova whom the prince was going to marry. She even went with her nanny to meet Tolstoy and plead with him to change the ending of the already published book, to not kill off Prince Andrei. In her extreme involvement with the characters from the novel, she seemed to echo my own story. For me, *Anna Karenina* had become something of an obsession. I was unable to come to terms with the tragedy of her life, and for a while, felt that I would never recover from the blow that fate had dealt her. I despised Tolstoy for having done this to her, and had there been a possibility of doing so, I would have dragged her away before she could come under the wheels of the train. Somehow Emma from *Madame Bovary*, even though she too committed suicide because of a failed affair, did not affect me in quite the same way.

But not long after, my anxiety shifted to Raskolnikov in *Crime and Punishment*. He had committed murder, and I kept dreading the moment when he would be caught. Was it immoral to feel sympathy for a murderer? I could see things from his point of view, to understand what had led him to kill the old woman, who seemed to be a mean and thoroughly despicable character. But did that make it okay for him to kill her? I felt morally challenged, unable to make up my mind about whether Raskolnikov was himself a loathsome person for having done what he had.

This sympathy for a criminal recurred in an even more intense form when I read Nabokov's compelling *Lolita*. I was haunted by the melancholy voice of the elegant paedophile narrator, Humbert Humbert. Even as, night after night, he abused the pubescent Lolita, I found myself unable to hate him. I could feel the intense emotion that had gripped him, and mesmerised by his voice, I forgave him, even though he evidently felt no remorse for what he had done. In fact, Lolita, whom he had robbed of childhood, came across as a pesky and rather annoying little brat. So, how did this shift in sympathy take place? Was it a conjurer's trick? From his point of view, and it was only his point of view that one was allowed to hear, his life, consumed as it was by his unquenchable, unrequited passion, had been deeply tragic. It was only on a recent re-reading of the book that I realised how unreliable a narrator Humbert was, and how persuasive his voice that had completely taken me in. What now emerged from the slippery text was Humbert's vileness, and Nabokov himself, in an interview, called him odious. Yet, in his extreme complexity—he was damaged and damaging, human and depraved, vengeful and brooding, deeply flawed and completely aware of being so—he was as inexplicable as life itself. It is not the business of literature to pass judgement. If a judgement is to be passed and a sentence given, it happens in the reader's mind. It didn't in mine. The text was exquisite, and the last line of the book has stayed with me:

> I am thinking of aurochs and angels, the secret of durable pigments, prophetic sonnets, the refuge of art. And this is the only immortality you and I may share, my Lolita.

Anthony Burgess's *A Clockwork Orange* again plunged me into a by now familiar moral crisis. Set in a dystopian, near-future England, the book had a reputation for its 'ultraviolence'. It was about the morality of free choice, about whether it is better to be conditioned to be good or to choose to be bad, and was written by Burgess in an invented argot called *Nadsat,* which had Russian and German loanwords. There was quite a bit of Shakespeare in the dialogues of the Beethoven-loving narrator, the teenaged Alex who indulged in street violence and had committed several heinous crimes. The *Nadsat* was a hard nut to crack, but when cracked, the book was utterly brilliant. The writing, even as it graphically described scenes of violence, was intensely lyrical. The whole crisis, of course, hinged on whether Alex deserved sympathy or not, and was excruciating precisely because of this; I just couldn't say.

Alice Munro, in 'Dimensions', suggested something of an answer. In the story, she got into the head of a 'criminally insane' father of three, who had murdered his young children in order to punish his wife. Munro hinted at how he, doing his time in a secure institution after he had committed the crime, might 'come out on the other side' at the end of much suffering and solitude, and even achieve a 'Grace'. She gave him a chance to present his side of things. In a 'document' to his wife, he wrote:

> What I Know in Myself is my own Evil. That is the secret of my comfort. I mean I know my Worst. It may be worse than other people's worst but in fact I do not have to think or worry about that. No excuses. I am at peace. Am I a Monster? The World says so and if it is said so then I agree. But then I say, the World does not have any real meaning for me. I am my Self and have no chance to be any other Self. I could say that I was crazy then but what does that mean? Crazy. Sane. I am I. I could not change my I then and I cannot change it now.

He went further to say that 'Heaven exists', that he had seen the children in another dimension, not the earthly one, and that they were 'really happy and smart'. This was the consolation that he held out to his wife. Was he insane? His wife did find in what he said 'a refuge'. It was not forgiveness but a kind of solace that she felt. And this solace had been given to her by the awful man who had murdered her children. No one else could quite understand what she felt. They were forever tied together by what had happened, and then, he was the only one now who remembered the children's names and the colour of their eyes.

It was in Delhi, when I started going to college, that I first noticed Kafka. He was there on the cover of his *Diaries 1910–23*, edited by Max Brod, that I found among my father's books on the living room sideboard of our Hauz Khas home. Kafka had his introspective gaze fixed on me. His straight nose and lips curved like the outspread wings of a bird had an austere beauty. I looked at him for the longest time, and it was love at first sight. Even more than love, he became a sort of idée fixe, and I set about moulding myself in his image. I put on a melancholy stance. I studied his handwriting in a page from the manuscript of the diaries that had been included in the edition owned by my father, and tried to form my letters like he did. I thought I was a tortured soul like him, because the way I wrote the letter F resembled the way in which he wrote his. I started writing a diary of my own, and tried to 'listen to myself outside of myself', as I found him doing in his diaries.

I read all his books that I could lay my hands on, though there was too much altogether to be read, and some of it was incomprehensible. More than his books, I was infatuated with the idea of Kafka. It seemed to me a miracle that short stories could be so very short, sometimes just a page long, or even a couple of sentences. I read incredulously his 'The Trees', which was exactly three and a half lines, and yet was a perfect story. In Willa and Edwin Muir's translation, it read:

> For we are like tree trunks in the snow. In appearance they lie sleekly and a little push should be enough to set them rolling. No, it can't be done, for they are firmly wedded to the ground. But see, even that is only appearance.

A friend, who knew of my obsession, gifted me *The Castle*. My father's copy of *Wedding Preparations in the Country* was tattered. I turned the pages gently, but they still fell apart; even the crumbling bits of brittle paper were too precious to be thrown away. I found a picture book of Kafka's *Prague* in the college library, and spent hours hidden behind the shelves, gazing at the cobbled streets of the city and at the scenes depicted in the black and white photographs on every page. I became a private eye, following Kafka wherever he went.

It was a couple of decades later that I came across the Urdu writer Naiyer Masud, and found in him an unexpected connection with Kafka. He loved Kafka as I did, and had translated some of Kafka's work into Urdu as *Kafka ke Afsane*. When I read Naiyer Masud's stories, I did not really find in them a Kafkaesque influence; it was more as if there was a similar imagination at work in both the writers, and perhaps this was why Masud had been attracted to Kafka, in the first place. I kept going back to Naiyer Masud's stories and often read the same ones over and over again—'Tahveel' (Transference), 'Itr-e-Kafur' (The Fragrance of Camphor), 'Nusrat', 'Vaqfa' (The Interval), 'Nudba' (Lamentation), all strange, dream-like and unsettling stories. What was it that compelled me to return to them again and again?

Here was a world that was meticulous in its detail, yet the details, instead of sharpening the images, seemed to make them less tangible. The scenes seemed very familiar to me. Had I been to those places and somehow forgotten them? Could I have dreamt them up? The stories were set in what seemed to be a familiar local qasba, but the qasba was not named, nor its location mentioned. Since Naiyer Masud lived in Lucknow, one might think that the place was perhaps Lucknow, but apart from one or two exceptions—'Ganjefa' (A Game of Cards), for instance—there was haziness about the locale that went against the grain of precision in the prose. It was only after a few readings that I realised that the qasba existed nowhere else but in the hermetic space that was the writer's mind. Yet in a mysterious way, that qasba seemed also to be located *within me*. I recognised the narrow, dark passageways with their half-open doors, the twisting by-lanes, the courtyards and arches, the empty rooms and dusty trees overhanging unused wells, as if I had seen them before; they felt like something at the edge of my consciousness. Yet I could not place them. Did they actually exist or were they just mental images? There seemed to be little distinction between the two. Always in sight but always elusive, the stories were like mirages.

Reading them became, for me, a kind of literary ventriloquism. The writer's voice was out there on the page, but it sounded as if it came from within me. I could not be the only one on whom the stories had this effect. Other readers too would have listened to their own distinct Masudian voice, and found their feet sinking into the shifting sands of the Masudian universe. I wanted to translate him, feeling drawn to him as he must have felt drawn to Kafka, when he translated him. I wanted others to read him, and yet I felt possessive, reluctant to let others enter that space which I felt was only mine. It took me a while to realise that Naiyer Masud deliberately suppressed identifiable markers, so that his stories seemed like half-remembered dreams. I found out later that some of the stories were, in fact, actual dreams that he had written down. In an interview with Asif Farrukhi, Masud said:

> What if one constructed the whole story, but didn't narrate the whole of it, not even hint at some of it—would it carry over to the reader's mind, however dimly? I soon realised that this was possible.

It was a valuable lesson in writing—so it was possible to remove large chunks of the narrative after they had been written down in great detail and still be able, after the excision, to convey the story. A few years ago, I found in Elizabeth Hardwick's genre-bending *Sleepless Nights,* which though entirely dissimilar to Masud's oeuvre in all other aspects, something of the same technique of omission. The descriptions, so dense and compressed that they even seemed to deny the term 'description', worked almost like aphorisms. They left out rather than left in. The withholding of clarity in Masud was a literary device, and it led to the feeling that something imperceptible was going on beneath the surface. In Hardwick, clarity was withheld because life itself was unclear, full of blanks and questions rather than answers.

Hardwick herself had a great love for reading. She said in a *Paris Review* interview:

> In reading certain works, not all works, I do sometimes enter a sort of hallucinatory state and I think I see undercurrents and light in dark places about the imagined emotions and actions.

It came to me that reading bleeds into writing and vice versa. That, as a writer, you bring to the text your own reading of it; you listen to the word with a hearing sharpened over a lifetime of writing, and each reading, with the passage of years, is a different reading. With a sort of Buddhist mindfulness, you follow the writer's voice that has behind it the weight of an entire life. And it reveals new ways of looking at the world.

It struck me that all my life I have been taking lessons in creative writing, and that these lessons have consisted only of reading. This is a course I signed up for when I was a child, and it has simply gone on. The vast textbook, much of it still unread, has chapters too many to count—

Mirza Hadi Ruswa, Sa'adat Hasan Manto, Shamsur Rahman Faruqi, Ismat Chughtai, Qurratulain Hyder, Intizar Husain, Premchand, Phanishwar Nath Renu, Rahi Masoom Raza, Krishna Sobti, Vinod Kumar Shukla, Agyeya, Nirmal Verma, Jyotsna Milan, Geetanjali Shree, Akhilesh, Dr Tulsi Ram, Sharatchandra, Mahashweta Devi, O.V. Vijayan, Vaikom Mohammad Bashir, M. Mukundan, Henry James, Carson McCullers, J.D. Salinger, Ernest Hemingway, Raymond Carver, Julio Ramon Ribeyro, Silvina Ocampo, Gabriel Garcia Marquez, J.M. Coetzee, Elizabeth Bishop, Clarice Lispector, Lydia Davis, Elsa Morante, Natalia Ginzburg, Elena Ferrante, Agatha Christie, Jean Rhys, Javier Marias, Italo Calvino, Italo Svevo, Dino Buzzati, Antonio Tabucchi, Olivia Laing, Gustave Flaubert, Guy de Maupassant, Honore de Balzac, Marguerite Yourcenar, Albert Camus, Annie Ernaux, Murasaki Shikibu, Yasunari Kawabata, Kazuo Ishiguro, Yukio Tsushima, Mavis Gallant, Alice Walker, Toni Morrison, Chinua Achebe, Willa Cather, Edith Wharton, Gerald Murnane, David Malouf, Peter Carey, Anton Chekhov, Ivan Turgenev, Ivan Bunin, Vladimir Nabokov, W.G. Sebald, Bruno Schulz, Thomas Mann, Jakob Wassermann, Bernhard Schlink, Jorge Luis Borges, Antonio di Benedetto, Fernando Pessoa …

The thing about this course is—it never ends.

Appendix
Four Stories

Zahra Rai
Mango Blossoms

I'd open the door myself whenever someone knocked. His way of knocking was different from anyone else's, but I felt pleasurably excited to think that it might be him. This happened every time there was a knock. In the time that it took me to get to the door, I thought about how I'd greet him if he was there. Would I smile or put on a sad face? Would I ask him where he'd been all this while or not? I also went to the door at the slightest sound because I was always waiting for him, every minute of the day; I thought about him all the time. My fear was that if a servant announced his arrival, Bi Amma, who'd be sitting right there, would send word that Bhaiyaji wasn't home, and he'd go away without coming inside or giving me a chance to set eyes on him. But if I brought him inside, she wouldn't be able to say very much and we could chat a little in Bhaijan's study.

I'd be disappointed even though I knew it wasn't him, and for a while I could not study or do anything else. Then I'd go and lie down in my room and think of all the possible reasons that could have kept him from coming.

Bi Amma was my grandmother and she was very fond of me. We too loved her because apart from her affectionate and trusting nature, she did not try to exercise undue control over us. She didn't mind my sitting around in the company of young men, flirting and playing cards with them, but when visitors asking after me looked embarrassed at seeing me surrounded by young men, she'd get worried too and once in a while tick me off. She did not approve of Bhaijan's friends coming inside the house in his absence, and how could I tell her that it was not Bhaijan that all of his friends came to see?

People at home had already begun to talk. They'd try their best to figure out what was going on, to see if they could read the story of my heart from my face. And I'd do my best to keep them guessing by treating all of Bhaijan's friends the same way. I was attracted to quite a few of them. To tell the truth, I was attracted to all young men. What, after all, was there in a young man for a girl to dislike? If I liked one for his masculine good looks, I liked another for the interesting things he said, and a third for his attractive voice. Each time I heard his voice, a shiver went through me, and I wanted him to speak again and again, so that I could experience the whole thing once more. There were other men I liked for their big American cars or television sets and refrigerators, and here age was no bar, nor looks—I didn't care if they had three chins. The only ones I disliked were those who remained indifferent to my blossoming youth and my beauty. The fact was that I liked all of Bhaijan's friends, for all of them were crazy about me. I, too, at least on the surface, gave none cause to despair. I'd sit in their midst like a doll, and my presence added such charm to the evening that before we knew it, it was two in the morning. Card games would be in full swing when Bi Amma called out—'Shami, come and sleep now, it's late.' But I went to my room only when the game had finished and everyone had left. I'd wake feeling pleasantly languorous, the spell of the previous evening still upon me. I didn't feel like going to the university and attending lectures, but if all of a sudden, he happened to turn up, my lassitude would disappear and I'd be a changed person, as though I'd become someone else. I found myself unable to walk slowly or speak without laughing, I felt as if I was flying. I had no need of anyone else when he was around; I was content to be with him. I knew that Bhaijan did not approve of the way I'd bet and play cards with him because he was a good player and won each time. He'd provoke me into betting large sums, I'd lose and keep emptying out Bhaijan's pockets. But I felt happy when I slid the pile of coins that I'd lost over to him, for it seemed to form a connection between us. And when he gathered up the money, I felt grateful, my heart softening even more towards him. It pleased me to lose against him.

I noticed that he didn't like me playing cards with anyone else, though he never said as much. He'd take my place at the game and ask me for some coffee. There'd be other times when he looked bored and started wandering about the room, scrutinising the knick-knacks. He'd view the painting on the wall or go up to the bookshelf, rest a knee on the carpet and look at the books. He'd fiddle with some fat books, but it was quite obvious from his distracted manner that he was simply turning the pages. He had a wheatish complexion, and with his thick hair falling over his forehead, he looked even more handsome. I loved the way he knelt down, dressed in his tightly fitting clothes.

'You're reading very seriously!' I teased him.

'Who's winning?' he asked, changing the subject.

I told him happily that I was, for I didn't like losing against anyone else. I became dejected too if he looked off-colour; he probably didn't know that I played with others simply to get an excuse to be where he was, not because I was interested in them. I finished with my deck of cards in rummy and smiled at Sohail.

'What, done already?' he asked.

'Well, what do you think!'

'Show me the sequence first.'

I showed him the sequence, then the run and the trail, and got up.

'I'll go get some coffee,' I said and left.

I put on the kettle and stood in front of the mirror. I was wearing a light lipstick. My face looked radiant, my eyes shone as though I'd just woken from a bewitching dream. My fine silken hair curled on my brow. I'm quite beautiful! I thought. He too must have seen my enticing lips, my shining eyes and my alluring smile. It was as if his lips came close to mine and I trembled—my ears began to burn and I had an intense desire to touch him.

Just then, the lid of the kettle began to rattle, startling me. The water had boiled. I poured it into the long-necked golden teapot that Bhaijan had brought from Japan, which was my favourite. It had a covering of rough wool and the long neck had an opening at the top. The lid's knob and the three legs of the pot were made of ivory. I took out this teapot only when I had a special guest.

When I entered the study with the jar of Nescafe and other items on a tray, I was relieved to find that Sohail had left. Rohit seemed to be dozing, bent forward on the writing desk. He opened his eyes when he heard me come in and looked at me without blinking—a long stare in which I read many things and again felt a shiver go through me. I lowered my eyes, embarrassed. He kept looking at me. I thought about how I must look to him as I went about fixing the coffee. He must have seen my slender hands and my shapely arms; I became aware that the deep purple blouse was tight on my arms and that my breathing had become rapid—was it possible for him to read my heart through my eyes? I felt a little worried.

Suddenly I heard him say: 'Will you come to the music conference at Rana's?'

'Alone?' I asked and at once became self-conscious. What would he have thought? Had I offended him? Surely there was no harm in going with him alone.

'No, your brother will also come, there's nothing to be afraid of,' he said and smiled.

Feeling like a fool I tried to save the situation: 'Who said I was afraid?'

'Then why did you ask if you'd have to come alone?' he asked with a hurt smile.

'Oh, I didn't mean to upset you! I just wanted to know if Bhaijan would come too. Isn't this your friend Rana who has a big house in Neelkanth Gali?'

'Yes, it's the same Rana who has a big house in Neelkanth Gali,' he mockingly imitated me and laughed.

'I've heard people say that Neelkanth Gali isn't safe!' I said.

'Well, it's true that the gali is a dangerous place ...' he teased me. 'Shami, just now you look like that frightened little schoolgirl whom ruffians abducted from the same Neelkanth Gali.'

I thought just then of the bird that flits restlessly, looking for a safe uninhabited and quiet place to build a nest in spring.

The prospect of going to the performance shut inside in a carriage, listening all the while to the sound of horses trotting was not my idea of a romantic outing. I've always despised the sound of hoofbeats and have never been fond of horses anyway.

I wanted to go on a rickshaw, for I could cuddle up to him on it—but, of course, I couldn't tell him this.

'What time will the programme begin? Shall I ask them to have the carriage ready?' Bhaijan asked and my heart sank, but I kept quiet.

'Why, aren't you coming? Why are you still in bed?'

'No yaar, I have a headache. Who knows how long the performance will go on for.'

'It could go on till 4 a.m. It'll be appropriate for him to close with an early morning Bhairavi—he'll probably sing his dadra, '*Chalo kahe ko jhuti banao batiyaan*....' You think the audience will let him leave without listening to this special piece of his?'

'Then the two of you had better go without me. Do ask for the carriage.'

'Two of you?' Again, a shiver went through me.

The lane was too narrow for a carriage, he told Bhaijan. Even a rickshaw could only go up till Kunj Gali, and then we'd have to walk. But what I wanted to know was whether he wanted to go on a rickshaw because he didn't have a choice or was it something else.

He hailed a rickshaw. It was Basant Panchami, the festival of spring, and in the excitement of listening to Raga Basant, I decided to wear a bright yellow sari that I thought would be appropriate for the occasion. It had turned cold; I put on a black cardigan. I stood in front of the full-length mirror when I had finished dressing. I don't know if my face was flushed because of the cold or due to the turmoil in my heart. I drew a thin line of kaajal in my eyes, extending the line a little beyond the corners of the eyes, and darkened my lipstick to enhance the colour. The cardigan, with the buttons fastened, emphasised the contours of my figure. I thought I looked ravishing. He was waiting for me outside and when he saw me, he said, delightedly. 'Ah! So, this really is a serious celebration of Basant!' I smiled and pretended to look shy as I climbed onto the rickshaw.

We'd come quite a long way. The wind was strong and my hand brushed against his.

'Your hands are so cold! Why, are you scared?'

'Not at all, do you take me for a coward?'

He didn't reply but spread out his heavy overcoat over my knees, and beneath it, he pressed my hand.

'I'll soon warm them up,' he said familiarly. He held my hand in a firm grip and so affectionately that I did not have the heart to take it away. He might get offended if I did, and I never could bear the idea of annoying him. It was as if he'd cast a spell on me. I began to tremble and my voice seemed to be sinking. 'It's very cold,' I said in a low voice.

He nestled closer and now we could feel the warmth of each other's bodies. My head dropped by itself onto his shoulder, and I felt my heart flutter as I got the intoxicating smell of his aftershave.

We reached Neelkanth Gali. We got off the rickshaw and walked to Rana's place. Rohit kept getting pushed against me in the crowd and each time he'd catch hold of my shoulders. The music hall was on an upper storey that was reached by climbing a narrow staircase. Guarding me like something precious, he escorted me upstairs.

The hall was full, so we had to sit close up against each other. I was still mesmerised. It felt so good to be sitting right next to him I quite forgot that the hall was full of people. I was aware only of him.

Soon Ustad Hafiz Ali Khan struck the first note on his sarod and I sat up. I wanted to soak in the music, each limpid note clear, like water. He started an alap in Raga Basant Bahar. The intricate interweaving of the two ragas, Basant and Bahar, was so melodious that the audience was enraptured. After playing for an hour, a thin stream of tears flowed from the ustad's eyes. The melancholy of spring pervaded the atmosphere. The spirit of the raga came alive and it was as if mango blossoms were raining down from the strings of the sarod. I wasn't sure what it was that kept twisting and throbbing within me. My imagination had become active and it was as if I saw miles upon miles of yellow mustard fields blooming. The hall seemed to be fragrant with mango blossoms. It was strange. I wondered at the deep connection of Indian classical music with the seasons; without a pre-written score or theme, the music seemed to contain the whole universe.

Right after the sarod, when Faiyaz Khan started on a lively Jaijaiwanti bandish, the mood of the audience changed and faces lit up. What a raga he'd chosen! It seemed to consist of those very emotions that we felt then; it certainly echoed mine. I could feel my fists clenching as the music scaled a peak. The vibrant notes seemed to shake up my nerves, which tingled with excitement at the surprises slowly revealed by the music. After singing for an hour, he doubled the tempo and started on '*Nadan ankhiyaan lagin*', playing around with the rhythm in his characteristic manner. Our heightened emotions became quieter. Rohit was now leaning so close onto my shoulder that I could feel his warm breath on my face. The ustad kept up a steady display of his wizardry with rhythm. The performance ended at 4 a.m. with Raga Bhairavi.

I felt drunk on the music I'd heard—the sadness of Basant Bahar and the restless Jaijaiwanti that was infused with the longing of separated lovers. We climbed down the stairs into the lane, which was pitch dark but for a light that glimmered in the distance. He took my hand again and I did not try to free it. I had no energy left after listening to the music.

We got into the rickshaw, and as it picked up speed, the air of that spring night seemed to me to be steeped in sorrow. The music had filled me with a sweet pain, and I felt a lump in my throat; it was as if there were tears and not blood flowing in my veins. This was probably because of Rohit's proximity, the few priceless moments that I'd got with him.

There was a blast of cold wind, and he wrapped a big woollen shawl around both of us. It seemed quite natural for us to be wrapped in the same shawl, and I felt carried away by the romance of it. I'd been brought up on conservative values, so the thrill that I felt on being so close to him was tempered by an anxious hesitation, though I could hardly tell him all this. Encouraged by my silence, he slipped his arm around my waist. I did not object. We were getting close to home. He cupped my face in both his hands and planted his lips on mine, which immediately felt crushed, burnt.

The rickshaw had reached the compound of the house and we alighted. I still felt intoxicated and my body seemed to be on fire. He looked serious and a little troubled. He glanced casually at my face, trying to read what I felt. I said nothing for a moment.

'What on earth came over you?' I asked, breaking the silence.

'Please forgive me, I should not have behaved as I did,' he said, anxiously running a hand over his forehead. I felt a stab of disappointment. Forgive? What was there to forgive? This wasn't at all what I was expecting. I felt like telling him 'You're an idiot. You haven't the least idea what a girl wants, have you?' But I couldn't bring myself to say this and he left.

I went to my room and collapsed on the bed. I don't know when I fell asleep, wondering whether he'd come again or had been frightened away by the encouragement offered by my ardent body.

(Originally published as 'Aam ke Baur' in *Dharmyug*, October 1969, collected in *Mahalsara ka Ek Khel aur Anya Kahaniyan*, ed. Sara Rai, Vani Prakashan 2020.)

Moghal Mahmood
The Will

Tahira had heard so much about Nishat Manzil that when she thought about it now, her mind conjured up scenes of beauty and happiness. She was sure that the joy the place exuded must once have been such as to make it seem like heaven. Along with this thought came another, that the deaths there would have been grand too. And as soon as she thought about death, her face would glow with joy.

Badi Begum was the most important person at Nishat Manzil. She had grown old and very weak. People dreaded even her minor indispositions. This time she was seriously ill. The medicines that usually helped her fever were proving ineffective. Hakeem Sahib tired of turning the pages of his books, but she did not recover. Even the best medicines did her no good. Tahira had always come to see her whenever she heard that the Begum was sick. She came this time too, and slowly she understood what was behind the silence that lay over Nishat Manzil. The trees seemed to be asleep in their deep shadows. A cold sadness was everywhere. She could not take her eyes off the Begum's pure innocent face. She felt that the Begum was shedding the green clothes of life and becoming denuded. In the glittering valuable tops that she wore in her ears, she saw the last flicker of the morning star, and the ring with the large gem that she wore on a finger of her right hand seemed to have lost its lustre, as though no longer belonging to it. A shiver would go through her when she saw the stamp of death on the Begum's face, and she'd smile to herself.

The night was dark and terrible. The atmosphere became even more ominous and frightening because of the howling of the street dogs. Tahira sat in her hovel, thinking. She had raised the wick of the lantern that had a blackened chimney. She could feel her heart beating in her chest. A blast of freezing wind set all the dogs howling together, and Tahira hastily shut the door. The chain of her thoughts was unbroken. She thought—this time, if Allah heard her prayers, she'd be able to do her duty by her daughter. The Begum Sahib was rich; alms would be distributed at her death. She'd be able to change the door of her hut; it was broken and she worried all night. The thought startled her. It was as if she was cursing the Begum, praying for her to die. But everyone had to die; there were so many desires in her heart that could only be fulfilled if someone were to die.

She lay awake through the night. She'd go out with the lantern at the slightest noise and then come back inside.

It must have been four o'clock in the morning when she heard someone calling out.

'Is Tahira Begum there?'

She started up and came to the door, holding the lantern with the blackened chimney.

'Who is it?'

The visitor said, 'I've come from Nishat Manzil.' He spoke haltingly, his voice choked with tears, 'Begum Sahib is dead. You've been summoned.'

Tahira sent him off after giving him an appropriate reply and then she lay there waiting for it to be morning, filled with pleasing dreams.

It was almost daybreak when Tahira left home, the city still asleep. Young, healthy-looking sweeper-women were out early, cleaning the streets. Doors were shut against the intense cold.

Tahira walked towards Nishat Manzil in long strides, wearing a black burqa. Her face bore that look of terrible calm which made people weep, for they knew what it meant. Her heart wanted to celebrate. She'd got the chance to work in a rich home after a long time. She could hear lamenting voices as she reached the big gate and she got the familiar smell of incense. She took off her burqa as soon as she came inside, decorously covered her head and moved to where the sounds were coming from. The crying voices settled on her soul like music.

Nishat Manzil looked desolate, burnt out and ashen. Despite the noisy lamentations of so many people, you could feel the silence. The Begum Sahib's daughters and other relatives were the loudest, creating quite a commotion. The doors of the Begum's room had been opened and she lay in eternal sleep on her high niwar bed with its soft mattress, covered with a sheet white as snow. There was a stream of mourners. Soon each corner of Nishat Manzil was crowded with people.

Tahira was sitting on the threshold, by the foot of the bed where the corpse lay. She'd covered her head with her white sari and held her face in both hands. At short intervals she'd speak out in measured tones, 'May Allah's name remain', and then she'd start examining the state of things around her. Sitting on a chair by the head of the corpse was a middle-aged woman with a divine expression on her face, reading aloud verses from the Quran. Her voice was thin and tuneful, her manner of rendering the Quran so affecting that the old women listening swayed to the rhythm and the arrested tears of the Begum's daughters began to flow again. A servant standing by swung a flywhisk over the body to make sure no flies settled on it. Tahira would occasionally take some incense glue from the box and put it in the fire, then she'd cover her face with both hands and listen to the Quran recitation. A rose-water sprinkler and some flowers lay on a stool, and the woman who was reciting the verses would now and again sprinkle some rose-water on the corpse.

Tahira remembered the incident from a few days ago, when she told her mother about a corpse she had recently bathed. It was so ghastly she couldn't get it out of her mind. She'd held both her ears and asked Allah's forgiveness for her sins. She imagined she saw that corpse again, lying on the ground. The big black ants in the ears and nose, the horrific blue face, the swollen stomach, as though it would burst the moment she touched it. 'Ya Allah, forgive me,' she said in a loud voice and her heart began to pound at the thought that she might be misunderstood. There was no way she could stop her thoughts. Ants came out each time she poured water on the face. She'd bathed innumerable corpses, it was nothing new for her, but she'd never seen one corpse so different from another. She kept thinking about the dreadful corpse she'd bathed recently and compared it to this one. The Begum Sahib's deeds were such that it seemed the doors of heaven were already open for her.

After weeping for long, the Begum's older daughter wiped her tears, swallowed a pill for energy along with a gulp of glucose, then looked at her sister and said, 'Sister, you'll kill yourself crying. Who will then do all the work that remains? Come on, pull yourself together. Saidani needs help with all the arrangements to be made. It's the last thing we'll be doing for our mother.'

The younger sister's tears started flowing again, and Saidani, going to the corpse, set up cries of 'Oh my Sarkar, oh my lady', loud enough to make the sky tremble, and the whole household began to shriek again.

Tahira got up and asked Saidani to be calm, and then she began to fill water for the bath and for washing the requisite utensils. She couldn't get that other corpse out of her mind, after which she'd seemed to see shadows of death in her own home. It all comes down to your deeds, she thought. Flowers rain down on the blessed when they die. What a sweet smell there was in the atmosphere here. It was written in the books that the places visited by the angels of mercy become perfumed like this. The dead woman looked splendid, as if she was sleeping and seeing beautiful dreams.

They'd filled a lot of water. Several large pots made of tin-plated copper were full, and there were the bowls and lotas also made of copper and similarly gilded with tin. Gram flour and jujube leaf paste had been kept at hand. No one except for Tahira and Saidani was allowed to touch the water, for none knew the intricacies of the last rites. This was the Begum's final bath and Allah would have to be answered to if standards of cleanliness and purity fell short.

Then Saidani wiped her tears and brought out the box in which the Begum had kept her shroud years ago. She'd written something on a piece of paper and kept that in the box too. For the last twenty years, the Begum had been taking care of this shroud. Each time she fell ill, she'd tell her daughters and Saidani, 'Look, before you begin my last rites, do open the box that has my shroud and read the paper I've put there, which is my will.' And during this illness in particular, she had told them, 'I'm not going to survive; don't forget what I said about the paper in the box.'

And everyone had spoken in one voice, 'God forbid! Why do you talk like this?' But the Begum closed her eyes and said, 'Death is inevitable. There is no escape from it.'

Saidani remembered her words in the midst of all the crying, but the cold was so intense that her hands wouldn't move. And one feels even colder in the presence of a corpse. Saidani had produced the box only when the sun was out and its light had spread everywhere.

Tahira's heart was pounding. A new mourner had come, and when the Begum's face was uncovered at her request, Tahira too went and stood there. She'd been anxious to scrutinise the body in the light of day. Those tops were still there in the Begum's ears. Her hands rested on her breast and the gem-studded ring on her finger glittered brightly. That was a relief. Tahira felt she was really lucky. What a woman the Begum was! Look at the arrangements she'd made before dying. It was only the pure-spirited who made arrangements for after they were gone. Tears of happiness welled up in her eyes and she wiped them, trying to give the impression that she'd burst into tears on seeing the Begum's face.

Saidani opened the box. The shroud had been folded carefully and wrapped in a waterproof wax-cloth. There was a sealed envelope on top, on which was written in big letters—'Read this first'.

Saidani brought the envelope to the daughters and said with the kindliness of an elder, 'Be patient dear ones, she was lucky that she had the two of you to leave behind in the world. Allah gave her no sorrows. Everyone has to die one day, but she was really fortunate that she suffered no torments while she was alive.'

Keeping up her narration, Saidani said, 'Here, read this first and then get started on the work. It'll be evening by the time we're done with the preparations. It's cold, the day is short and our Sarkar has a long way to go.'

The girls began to cry again. Saidani lovingly said, 'Come on, stop crying and get on with your duty; this is the day for which one has children.'

News came in that Maulana had come. The bustle of the house increased. Tahira rolled up the sleeves of her old but warm jacket to her elbows. She tidied her hair, tightening it into a small plait, and got ready, sari wrapped around her waist. She'd been in a similar state of preparedness to bathe corpses many times in her life. But she'd never before felt such an eagerness to begin work.

Outside, Maulana said a prayer for the dead woman, talked a little about her and sent word inside that they should hurry with the essential work.

When the older daughter got up and took the warm shawl off her head, many silver strands shone out from her thick beautiful hair. She cast a glance at the gathering, and holding out the envelope to the woman who'd been reading the Quran, said, 'Please read this out loudly so that everyone may hear.'

The woman opened the envelope and began to read aloud. Everyone fell silent and listened.

1) That if there is sunshine available, my shroud should be spread out in the sun for a while.

2) That only the twenty-five gold coins kept in the shroud should be used for my last rites; no other money should be used.

Wah! Wah! There were approving noises. Such wisdom! No ordinary mind can think of these subtleties. People had their eyes fixed on the reader. Tahira's anxiety was growing. The woman read on:

3) That whoever bathes me should be given the jewellery on my body and my bed, along with the bedding.

The woman put down the paper, and now that they'd heard the will, the daughters stopped weeping. There was no particular effect on Saidani, but energy shot through Tahira's body like a current and her face began to shine.

Saidani got up and spread the shroud on a white sheet in the sun. She put away the wax-cloth in the empty box, counted out the twenty-five gold coins and handed them over to the older daughter.

There were long quotations from the Quran written in beautiful letters with saffron ink on the shroud. Some of the women who'd come picked up their children and moved away.

Setting out the things needed for the bath, Tahira made a mental estimate of the ring and the ear-tops. She'd be able to make the best arrangements for her daughter's wedding with so much money. Allah willing, she'd discharge her duty this year itself. It was not good to keep a grown daughter at home. May Allah grant the Begum Sahib heaven; it was so kind of her to have left a will. A curse would befall those who ignored the wishes of the dead. It was her beneficence that lit up the dead face, as though there were a lamp shining within her.

The water containers were being moved around, the gram flour and camphor mixed in bowls. Between Tahira and Saidani on one side and the two sisters on the other, they placed the Begum's body, graceful even in death, on the wooden bed. This led to another burst of crying and some people stepped away. Saidani and Tahira readied themselves to begin.

Just then, the older sister thought of something. She called out to the younger sister and said to Saidani, 'Saidani, wait, don't touch her yet. We're going to do this last service for her with our own hands. It's not as if we're going to get another chance. Come, there's nothing to cry about, it's your duty.'

Tahira felt the ground slide from beneath her feet and darkness came over her. Those dreams she'd nurtured for so long, what would become of them? And what of her daughter? All her plans turned to ash, her desires were washed away.

The sisters touched a dead body for the first time in their lives with trembling hearts. They'd never even seen a corpse from so close. The younger one kept crying throughout. The ring and the tops were taken off carefully, the rites completed.

The white shroud, elegantly inscribed with saffron ink, seemed to heighten the glow on the Begum's face.

There was such a commotion when the Begum was given her last farewell that earth and sky seemed to quake.

Tahira got one copper lota, one bowl, the Begum's bedding, a quilt and ten rupees, Saidani the other lota and bowl, the niwarbed, a warm shawl and ten rupees.

It was ten o'clock when Tahira came home, and incredibly cold. It was one of the last nights of the moon. There was deep darkness and from far away came the sound of dogs howling.

Tahira reeked of camphor. Her hair was loose. The door was opened when she knocked, and she sat down on the floor in a corner of the hut, trembling with cold and grief.

Tahira's old mother was sitting on the bed dozing, and a girl of fifteen or sixteen slept beside her. The mother gave Tahira a subdued look, for she knew what the strong smell of camphor meant. She drew a blanket over the girl and dozed off again.

Tahira did not speak to her mother; she glanced at her sleeping daughter and closed her eyes. Her pale face looked even paler. It was as if there were ants crawling inside her head. She seemed to see spectres of death in the terrible loneliness of the night. The dogs, frozen in the cold, continued to howl. There was a raw wind blowing; she felt benumbed, paralysed.

(Originally published as 'Vasiyatnama' in *Kahani*, January 1961, collected in *Mahalsara ka Ek Khel aur Anya Kahaniyaan*, ed. Sara Rai, Vani Prakashan 2020.)

Shivrani Devi
The Holi of Ruin

Ever since the Holi on which his son was born, the year Nirmalchand turned forty, his wife Uttama had begun to celebrate the festival with much fervour. The preparations would begin months ahead. The tailor would get busy stitching clothes, the halwai with making sweets, and the house would be decorated. A dance room would be set up for the revelry. The merry-making began right from Basant. Alms were generously given to the poor. Three more sons had been born since the first one, and Holi became an even bigger affair. It was no longer simply a festival; the day had become sacred. And each year something new was added to the festivities. A play would be performed or clothes distributed to the poor. Sometimes half a year's interest would be waived on sums owed by the peasants. Nirmalchand was a kind landlord who now and then also gave donations.

It was the month of Magh, the end of winter. Nature had opened its box of scents and colours. Nirmalchand returned from his fields that were green with the new shoots of spring, and said to Uttama, 'Did you know that Basant is almost here? Upadhyayji just told me.'

Nirmalchand never remembered dates or months. He knew that the sun rose in the east, but he'd never been able to figure out the moon of Pariwa or of Purnamasi. He was educated and, in his youth, had been inclined to write poetry. He still kept up with the current trends in politics.

Uttama was preparing a paan for him, 'Really?' she said, 'Now that's interesting. Tomorrow is Basant.'

Nirmalchand got worried. 'Yes, and I had not an inkling. Now tell me, what are we to do?'

Uttama was a walking calendar and knew her dates. She had no education but was skilled in dealing with household matters.

She feigned ignorance and said, 'This is difficult. Didn't you scold Upadhyayji? He really should have told us earlier.'

'And you too did not remember?'

'No. I was relying on you.'

'You know me—I'm an idiot.'

'Well, if that lets you off the hook, then consider me mad too.'

'You, mad? I was an idiot, but I wouldn't have remained one if I thought you were mad! It's all because of you that I'm so useless. I stopped worrying about these things when I saw that you could manage without my help. What I fret about is money. I bought a life insurance policy just yesterday and sent them three hundred rupees for the first installment. And I paid an advance on the furniture as well. I could have put all this off for a few months, if you'd only mentioned Basant was coming. And now I haven't a clue about what's to be done. It's up to you to handle it all; I wash my hands of it.'

Uttama laughed and said, 'It's okay, don't worry your head about it. I'm not like you that I'd have no idea of Basant. I don't need you to tell me. I've already made arrangements. Now won't you thank me for the favour I've done you?'

Nirmalchand's worries evaporated. Pleased, he said, 'Why should I? Holi's given you children and it's for you to celebrate it. I don't need to thank you. Besides, they cling only to you; they start crying when I try to play with them.'

'Well, honestly! Why don't you admit that it's you who has no time for them? It's no joke keeping children amused. They can tell who's interested in them and who isn't.'

'I was born a fool and you've made me worse. On top of that, I have to put up with your taunts!'

'One sure could learn from you how to wheedle and cajole!'

Suddenly the earth started trembling like a leaf. It was a terrible earthquake. The couple had been indulging in banter one minute, and the next there was panic. Nirmal looked worried. 'What's going to happen now? Looks like the house will collapse.'

'You take the boys and run. Go to the fields. Where is Bhal? Find him too. I'll try and save some things from the house.'

Nirmalchand had just started out with the three children when the courtyard split wide open and all four of them fell into the crack. Uttama ran out screaming and the wall collapsed upon her.

Bhalchand was playing outside. He saw the house falling and ran, calling out to the servants. For half an hour it grew quite dark and except for cries of help nothing could be heard. When the dust settled, they found an unconscious Uttama buried under the rubble. Nirmalchand and the three children had been interred in the bowels of the earth. The carefree home was destroyed within minutes.

When Uttama came to, she found herself in a hut. Bhalchand was sitting by her, crying.

Uttama cried out, 'Water! Give me some water!'

Bhal wiped his eyes and poured some water into her mouth. 'How are you feeling, Amma?' he asked.

Uttama looked at him with vacant eyes. 'I'm fine, but where am I, Bhal? And where are your father and the children?'

Bhal sobbed and said, 'The earthquake has gobbled them all, Amma. There's nothing more to say. God's swallowed them.'

'God help us!' exclaimed Uttama. 'What's this you're telling me?' And she fainted again.

It was almost Holi. Instead of the deafening sound of music and firecrackers, there was silence. The ground that would turn red with abir and gulal was being watered with tears. Laments had taken the place of Holi drums and songs.

Yet, Uttama was preparing to celebrate Holi. She had smeared her hut with cow-dung and spread some tattered mats in front of the door. She hadn't prepared the usual delicacies but had made baatis instead, and was going about the village trying to bring some cheer—'Come on, let's do the Holi puja together. Those who died have gone to God and must be relishing the joys of heaven. So why should we, who've been left behind, grieve? Show the ones up there that we don't give a fig for the wounds they've inflicted!'

People heard what she said and were sad for her. They tried to console her. Some cried and others laughed; they said she had lost her mind. It's all God's doing. They cursed him and doubted his existence. There is no God. Nature would run its course without caring who lived or died. If God could not protect them, why should they take his name? Uttama had lost her family and possessions, what was there now to pray for?

Bhalchand said, 'That's how it is, Amma. Festivals are for when the house is full of loved ones. What good is Holi when everyone's in mourning?'

The mother gave her son a look of affectionate disdain.'What kind of talk is this, son? The rich man does not value money—but ask those who have just enough for one meal! Who cares to please the gods when the home is full of people? But when there are so few left that if you lost them too, you'd have no reason to live, it's natural for you to guard them with your life. Keep your eyes on the future, son. What's the point of regretting what's already happened? Don't mourn what's lost, celebrate what remains. How could Bhal or anyone in the village understand what it cost the sorrowing mother to keep her grief in check?

At midnight, when Uttama set out to light the Holika fire, singing as she went, everyone in the village was with her. They'd begun to believe in her. She had got the better of misfortune and that made her a goddess. Uttama went round the fire when it was blazing. The village folk walking behind her were deeply moved and had tears in their eyes as they chanted,

'*Mata humko do vardan, jisse hamara ho kalyan!*' (Bless us, mother, so that we may prosper!)

When the Holika fire had died out, Uttama put a pinch of ash on every forehead and prayed to Holi Mata: 'Mother, protect these children of yours. Many sacrifices have been made to you; ask for no more from them now. If you're going to take away all whom we love, who then will we live for? If you have to, then take all of us. Why carry away some, and leave the others behind to grieve?'

Uttama had grown large-hearted. The difference for her between those who were hers and those who weren't had been erased. She loved them all as if they were her children.

The next morning was Holi. There was festivity everywhere. Uttama went round by turns to all the houses saying—'Brothers and sisters! Sing and make merry! Why weep over those who've gone? Be glad for those who are still around and give them your blessings.'

The whole village gathered in front of Uttama's hut in the evening and the joy of this year's Holi surpassed that of other happier ones. The space fallen vacant in her heart was filled again in the auspicious flow of goodwill.

(Originally published as 'Vidhvans ki Holi' in Shivrani Devi's short story collection, *Kaumudi*, Saraswati Press, 1937, reprinted Nayee Kitab, 2020.)

Premchand
Ramlila

It's been ages since I last saw a Ramlila. The sight of men screaming *Hoo! Hoo!* and running around in crude monkey masks, knee-length pajamas and short black shirts seems ridiculous. The Ramlila of Banaras is known the world over, and people travel great distances to see it, but it is much like any other Ramlila performed anywhere else. I too would go to see it and have to admit that it had some good stage props. The masks that the demons and the monkeys wore were made of brass, and so were their maces. Perhaps the exiled brothers wore crowns that had real gold in them, but that did not make the performance less absurd. The crowds turned up regardless.

There was a time when I enjoyed the Ramlila, though that's an understatement. It was more like an obsession. I was fortunate that I lived close to the Ramlila ground, and the house where the actors were made up for the performance was right next door. The make-up proceedings began at two in the afternoon, and I'd be there from the start, eager to run any errands I was asked to. I cannot muster the same enthusiasm today even when I go to collect my pension. The make-up of the princess was done in one of the smaller rooms. Yellow clay was smeared all over her body; powder was applied to her face, and small red, green and blue dots were put across her forehead, cheeks and chin, making her look like a piece of decoration. There was only one man who was good at this, and he'd do the three main actors by turns. It was my job to get water for the mixing bowls, to grind the yellow earth, and to fan the actors.

Once the preparations had been completed, the chariot carrying the Ramlila performers was taken out. Today when I attend his Lordship's durbar, I don't feel the same pride that I felt then, sitting behind Ramchandraji on the chariot. The only time I came close to it was when the home member seconded a proposal of mine in the management committee. A similar wave of excitement went through me when my elder son was nominated for the post of deputy sub-collector. But there's still a big difference between these occasions and the bliss that I felt in childhood. It was as if I was in heaven.

It was the day when the boatmen performed their Ramlila. I'd been tempted into a game of gulli-danda and had missed the make-up. The chariot appeared, but I still didn't abandon the game. I was hell-bent on playing my turn; I did not have the requisite quality of self-sacrifice to forgo it. If I'd been the one slogging, I'd have run away long ago. But making others slog is something else. Anyhow, my turn was over soon. There was room enough to cheat and carry on for another few minutes, but this was not the time for it. I ran to the canal. The chariot had reached the water's edge. I could see from afar the mallah bringing in the boat. It was difficult to run through that crowd. Finally, pushing through with sheer force of will, I reached the ghat to find that the boatman had already left.

I had such faith in the boy who played Ramchandra! I neglected my own studies to coach him so that he wouldn't fail. Even though he was older than me, he was in a lower grade. But the same Ramchandra was sailing off in the boat with his face turned away as if he didn't know me. An actor often imbibes the qualities of the character he is playing. Why would Ram, known for the harsh eye he cast on his devotees, make an exception for me? I began to jump about agitatedly, like a calf who feels the yoke on its neck for the first time. I'd leap towards the canal and then run back looking for someone who could help me. But people were busy enjoying themselves and my cries were not heard. I've had my share of troubles since then, but nothing matches the distress I felt that day.

I resolved never to speak to Ramchandra or give him tasty tidbits to eat. But as soon as he crossed the canal and returned, I clambered happily onto the chariot as if nothing had happened.

2

The Ramlila was over. The enthronement ceremony was about to take place, but it was taking a long time. Perhaps enough money hadn't been collected. No one now cared for Ramchandra. He was given nothing to eat and he didn't get a break so that he could go home and have a bite. Around three o'clock Chaudhari Sahib sent some food across. For the rest of the day, no one bothered to get him even a glass of water. But my faith in him remained the same. As far as I was concerned, he was the same Ramchandra. If I got hold of something nice to eat, I'd go and give it to him. Instead of eating it myself, I got more pleasure from feeding him. I'd run to the chaupal as soon as I had a sweet or a fruit, and if Ramchandra wasn't there, I'd search for him. I couldn't rest till I'd found and fed him.

The day of his accession to the throne arrived. A big canopy had been put up in the Ramlila ground. Courtesans, too, came in groups. Ram's chariot was taken out on its rounds in the evening and was met at each door with arti. Depending on the faith they had in him, people gave him a rupee or a few paisas. My father was a police officer and performed the arti without giving any money. I cannot describe the shame I then felt. I happened to have on me a rupee that my uncle had given me when he visited us during Dussehra. I'd put it by and couldn't spend it even on the day it was Dussehra. I now put the rupee in the arti thali and Pitaji could only glare angrily at me. He said nothing, but his expression made it clear that I had disgraced him. It was almost ten o'clock at night by the time Ramchandra's rounds were done. The arti thali was full of notes and coins. I can't say for sure but there must have been at least four or five hundred rupees on it. However, Chaudhari Sahib had spent more than this on the festivities and was keen to raise another two hundred at least. He thought the best way to do this would be to use the courtesans. Once people were seated and the mehfil had warmed up, Abadijan, using her skills of coquetry, was to embarrass the dance-lovers in the audience into parting with their money. There was a discussion between Chaudhari Sahib and Abadijan, and I happened to listen in. Chaudhari Sahib must have thought that I was too young to understand what was going on. But by the grace of God, I was the very image of intelligence, and was on to the plan at once.

Chaudhari said, 'Listen Abadijan, isn't this a bit much? It's not as if our paths have crossed for the first time. God willing, you'll keep coming here. The collection's fallen short this time or I wouldn't have insisted.'

Abadi replied, 'Look at you, trying your zamindari on me! But I won't let you get away with it this time. I'm supposed to rake in the dough while you sit there twirling your moustache! That's a fine way to make money. You'll be a king in no time. What's a zamindar compared to a king? Why, you could set up a bordello and just watch the money flow in.'

'You're teasing me when I'm already in a tight spot.'

'Well, you're trying your tricks on me too. But it's all in a day's work for me, to make cunning people like you dance to my tune.'

'All right, what is it that you want?' asked Chaudhari.

'We'll go halves on whatever I make. Come, give me your hand. It's a deal.'

'Fine, have it your way.'

'First hand me my hundred rupees. What if later you go back on your word?'

'So you want money now, as well as afterwards!'

'Did you really think I wouldn't charge extra for this? So now I see your game! I should have known. You pretend that money has no meaning for you, but look how cunning you become as soon as your own money is involved!'

'Are you bent upon extracting a double fee?'

'I'm doing this only because you want me to do more than we'd agreed upon. I'd have been happy just to get my hundred rupees. It's not as if I like reaching into people's pockets.'

There was no way Chaudhari could win. He had to give in to Abadi. The dance began. Abadi was a vivacious woman. She was so youthful and ravishing, and had such a captivating manner, that I too felt myself coming under her spell. She had a knack for recognising her prey. She'd sit down in front of her quarry and not let go until she had extracted some money from them. I don't think there would have been anyone who gave her less than five rupees. To my embarrassment, she came up to Pitaji as well. When she caught hold of his wrist, I dreaded he would jerk her hand away and perhaps snub her too—but what was this? Dear God, were my eyes playing tricks on me? Pitaji was smiling behind his moustache! I'd never seen such a sweet smile on his face. His eyes were brimming over with love and each pore of his body seemed to exude happiness. But God saved my face. There he was, gently freeing his wrist from Abadi's hands. But no, what was it now? Abadi had put her arms round his neck! He'd surely hit her this time. The witch had no shame.

One gentleman smiled and said, 'You'll get nothing here, Abadijan! Go look to someone else.'

What he'd said was exactly what I'd been thinking too, and it was the proper thing to say. But Pitaji looked at him with angry eyes and twirled his moustache. Though he said nothing, the expression on his face seemed to shout, 'You bania! What did you take me for? I'm ready to give my life for something like this; and you're talking about money! Go on, try me. I won't show my face again if I pay less than double the sum you would.'

It was a scandal! Why didn't the earth split, the sky fall down? Why didn't I die? Pitaji took something from his pocket and, showing it to Sethji, gave it to Abadijan. Ah, it was an asharfi! Everyone clapped. Sethji looked like such a fool. I couldn't make up my mind whether Pitaji had won or lost. All I'd seen was him giving a gold coin to Abadijan. He looked thrilled and proud of himself, as if he'd been even more generous than the legendary Hatim, known for his generosity. This was the same man who looked as if he'd rip me apart when he saw me put a rupee in the arti thali. I'd done what the occasion demanded, and this had put a slur on his prestige. And here he was, bursting with pride at this hateful, revolting exchange.

Abadijan met the gesture with a salaam and a heartwarming smile before she moved on. I could sit there no longer. I couldn't raise my head for shame; if I hadn't seen it all with my own eyes, I'd never have believed it. Usually, I reported all I'd seen outside to Amma, but I kept this to myself, knowing it would hurt her.

The singing went on the whole night. I could hear the thump of the tabla. I was tempted to go out and see it all, but I couldn't face it. What if someone started talking about Pitaji?

Ramchandra was to leave early the next morning. I got up, still rubbing my eyes, and ran to the chaupal, fearing he might already have gone. The carriages for the courtesans were ready to leave. They were surrounded by scores of people looking longingly at them. Without so much as a glance at them, Imade straight for Ramchandra. Lakshman and Sita were in tears, and Ramchandra, with his lutiya on a string across his shoulder, was trying to console them. Except for me, there was no one there. I asked in a choked voice, 'Is your bidai done?'

Ramchandra replied, 'Yes, it's done, but what does it amount to? Chaudhari Sahib says "Now go" and we leave.'

'Didn't you get any money or clothes?'

'No, nothing yet; Chaudhari Sahib said he's made a loss. He's asked us to come later for the money.'

'You got nothing at all?'

'Not one paisa. I was hoping to buy some books. But we didn't even get the fare to go back. You don't have far to go, he said. You can walk.'

I felt so angry that I wanted to go to Chaudhari Sahib straight away and give him a piece of my mind. There was enough money and carriages for the courtesans, but nothing at all when it came to Ramchandra and his companions! The same people who'd showered ten- and twenty-rupee notes on Abadijan had not even a few annas for them? Pitaji too had given Abadijan a gold asharfi; now I wanted to see what he would give Ramchandra. I ran to him. He was ready to go out on an investigation. He saw me and asked, 'What are you doing here? It's time to study and all you can think of is loafing about!'

'I've just been to the chaupal,' I said. 'Ramchandra is leaving and Chaudhari Sahib has given him nothing.'

'So how does that concern you?'

'How is he to go home? He hasn't even been paid the fare!'

'What, not even the fare? This is so unfair of Chaudhari Sahib!'

'If you give me just two rupees, I'll give them to him. They might be enough to see him home.'

Pitaji looked at me sharply. 'Go read your books. I have no money.'

Even as he spoke, he climbed onto his horse to leave. After that, I lost respect for him and stopped heeding his scolding. I felt he no longer had the right to teach me anything. The mere sight of him irritated me and I did the opposite of whatever he told me to do. This did me no good, but then I was full of defiance.

I still had two annas, and I hesitantly gave them to Ramchandra. His joy at seeing the money was beyond my expectations. He fell upon it like a thirsty man getting water.

The two annas were all that the three deities went away with. I was the only one who saw them off till the edge of the qasba.

I returned with tears in my eyes, but my heart was full of joy.

(Originally published as 'Ramlila' in *Madhuri*, 1926.)

Acknowledgements

'On Not Writing' (as 'You will be the Katherine Mansfield of Hindi') was first published in *The Caravan* and subsequently in *The Book of Indian Essays: Two Hundred Years of English Prose*, edited by Arvind Krishna Mehrotra (Black Kite/Hachette India, 2020). 'Mango Blossoms' and 'The Will' appeared in *The Silence that Speaks: Short Stories by Indian Muslim Women*, edited by Haris Qadeer (Oxford University Press, 2022). Acknowledgements are due to the editors.

I'm grateful to Karthika VK and Minakshi Thakur for their editorial support and enthusiasm; to Mita Kapur for her help and friendship; to Anil Rai for making the Danish edition of *Godan* available to me; to Seema Segal for family discussions and shared childhood memories; and to Alok Rai for providing important details about our grandparents and the Godowlia house in Banaras. I thank him too for his affection and concern. Thanks are due to Hashim Raza Ali Bakht for details about the Nawab-ki-Deorhi family, and to Mehdi Bakht for the Hindu branch of the family tree; to Zafar Bakht for making possible a visit to the family graveyard at Karbala, Allahabad. Aslam has been a reassuring presence, and I cannot thank him enough. Arvind Krishna Mehrotra and Lara Ahsan Chandni have been with me throughout the writing of this book. They were its first readers and it is to them this book is dedicated.